Incisive Journalism In Cameroon: The Best of "Cameroon Report" (1978 – 1986)

Edited By
Michael Sam-Nuvala Fonkem

Langaa Research & Publishing CIG
Mankon, Bamenda

Publisher:
Langaa RPCIG
Langaa Research & Publishing Common Initiative Group
P.O. Box 902 Mankon
Bamenda
North West Region
Cameroon
Langaagrp@gmail.com
www.langaa-rpcig.net

Distributed in and outside N. America by African Books Collective
orders@africanbookscollective.com
www.africanbookcollective.com

ISBN: 9956-791-17-2

© Michael Sam-Nuvala Fonkem 2014

DISCLAIMER
All views expressed in this publication are those of the author and do not necessarily reflect the views of Langaa RPCIG.

The Editor

Michael Sam-Nuvala Fonkem is an accomplished journalist who has been practicing uninterrupted since graduating in 1976 from the International School of Journalism, Yaoundé (Ecole Suprieure de Journalisme de Yaoundé-ESSIJY). His professional career which kicked off as a news anchor and commentator at the National Station of Radio Cameroon, Yaoundé brought him face to face with the grim reality of the consequences of refusing to play the role of 'His Master's Voice'. Interrogations with the 'political police', intimidations, arrests and a 5-month spell of incarceration at the Nkondengui maximum security prison, Yaounde was the price he had to pay for being a free thinker.

From 1987 -1990, he taught journalism at his alma mater (now known as ESSTIC) where the authorities believed it was safer to contain him than the Radio but he fell out with the School's Director and was later sent on internal administrative exile to the Adamawa Province (now Region) as Provincial Chief of Media Monitoring, a post he promptly rejected. During his journey through the wilderness marked by a lay-off from the Cameroon Civil Service in 1998, Sam-Nuvala Fonkem wrote for a number of news publications until he joined the United Nations Operation in Cote d'Ivoire (UNOCI) as Public Information Officer in 2010.

Contributors

Wilfred Nkwenti

Mark Niboh

Tatah Mentan

Shey Peter Mabu

Fai Henry Fonye

Luke Ananga

Eric Chinje

Victor Epie Ngome

George Ngwa

Ben Bongang

Charles Landzeh

Akwanka Joe Ndifor

Ngobesing Romanus

Adamu Musa

Vincent Azobi

Ebssy Ngum

Julius Wamey

Sam-Nuvala Fonkem

Dedication

This book is for:

Mark Niboh, Achidi Difang of the celebrated *Cause for Concern* program of Radio Douala, Fai Henry Fonye, Luke Ananga, Charles Landzeh, Akwanka Joe Ndifor, Ebbsiy Ngum, George Tanni, Sammy Anguh and all the valiant Anglophone men and women of Radio Cameroon who have passed on since the beginning of the fight for freedom of speech.

Your legacy is a source of consolation and by far compensates for the thanklessness encountered in the journalism profession in Cameroon.

Table of Contents

1. The C.N.U: Twelve Years After...1
2. Cameroon Report 18/1/81: Wum Farmer-Grazier Problem..3
3. A chaotic Highway Transporters Union..........................7
4. Inhuman prison conditions...11
5. Lay Private Education..15
6. Health for all by year 2000..19
7. Catering for disabled persons..23
8. Cameroon Nigeria Reconciliation....................................27
9. The Role of our Parliamentarians....................................29
10. Wastage and Mismanagement in Public Health Services..33
11. Crackdown on Customs Fraud....................................... 37
12. FONADER: Not yet the Farmer's Bank....................... 41
13. Mount Cameroon Erupts..45
14. President Ahmadou Ahidjo's Dramatic Resignation......49
15. The Task Ahead for President Paul Biya........................53
16. Biya and the Housing Crisis..57
17. Our Ailing Parastatal Corporations................................ 61
18. The University as Brain Trust... 65
19. Biya on Housing and Road Construction......................69
20. April 6 Coup Attempt: An Appraisal..............................73
21. In the Dawn of the Abortive Coup................................77
22. Reflection on May 20...79
23. Parastatal Corporations Revisited...................................81
24. Chasing Files: A Product of Centralisation...................85
25. The Plight of our Farmers.. 89
26. The One-shift and Two-shift Working systems.............93
27. Decentralisation versus Decongestion............................97

28. 13th Anniversary of the Unitary State..................99
29. The Role of Development Committees..................103
30. 1985 Budgetary Session..................107
31. MUNA on Bilingualism..................109
32. The Concept of Development Journalism..................113
33. The Question of Certificate Equivalence..................115
34. Harmonising Our Two Legal Systems..................119
35. The First October Story..................123
36. May 20th: Our Dream of a New and Great Cameroon..127
37. The CPDM and Civil Liberties..................133
38. Enemies of Democracy..................137
39. Towards a New World Information Order..................145
40. Africa's Five Million Refugees..................149
41. Boycotting sporting links with Racist South African.....153
42. The Proposed Senegambian confederation..................157
43. The I.M.F. Tightens policy towards Third World..........161
44. The Assassination of SADAT: Consequences on Egyptian Politics..................165
45. The North-South Dialogue..................169
46. Ciskei Homeland: Another stride for Apartheid..........173
47. Palestinian Autonomy..................177
48. Cameroon's Position on SADR'S Admission into the O.A.U..................181
49. The 9th Franco-African Summit..................185
50. OAU Deadlock over Western Sahara..................189
51. Foiled OAU Summit Reconvened..................193
52. Checking the African Dependency Syndrome..................197
53. The O.A.U. Drought Fund..................203
54. The Western Sahara Ten Years After..................207
55. South Africa: Botha's Lame Reforms..................211
56. African Leaders in Europe..................215
57. South Africa's puppet Government in Namibia..........219

58. Africa's Troubled Politics..223
59. Pope John Paul II in Africa... 227
60. Leadership Succession in Africa..231
61. Reagan-Gorbachev Summit...235
62. Africa and its Elections..239

Preface

This selection of news commentaries and analyses is in itself so good, and so fairly represents the spirit, purpose and quality of Cameroon Report as to need explanation by way of introduction. The selection could have been titled Voices of Dissent in the context of our times and the background of its libertarian heritage.

However, we sharply differ at many points of diagnosis and cure of social evils unanimously believed to be inevitable in human progress writ large. That is why we avoided claiming mantles of Godly wisdom, naively, thinking that we dwelt in a world of life without sorrows, frustrations and problems. Hence, we, of different intellectual persuasions, all had our nostrums to heal society of greed, poverty, political fraud, corruption, war, repression and pigheaded leadership in Cameroon and beyond.

These prescriptions are all relatively simple. Cameroonian, African or any other human being if not infinitely perfectible by theological standards, is infinitely educable to his own true interests. Error and crime against humanity are wholly the fault of man's social, political and economic environment. And no worthy journalist can afford to give mere verbal homage to human dignity.

Many of the dwindling number of self-proclaimed African "Father(s) of the Nation" have hardly been realistic. These tin gods have been unblinking enemies of the forces of democracy; they have been presiding over the liquidation of their nations; they have been the true thieves of state! And they have been killing their citizens mindlessly in the comfort of a theologian who consoles himself that anyhow he would meet his fellow believers of the enemy camp in heaven.

The Cameroonian society in particular is a society of the minority, i.e. minority ruling groups, in a continent half of whose people live on the borderline between hunger and starvation. Such a country sorely needs wisdom more appropriate to it than any which we have inherited from our speech addicts since independence in 1960. That wisdom will be born of intelligent dissent and the avoidance of premature orthodoxies.

But the lasting merit of this book is that its dissent is constructive. It is neither a dissent of negative despair nor of brittle cynicism.

The range of these commentaries and analyses is wide. It is concerned with the whole man rather than any political creed. But the writers, whose labour is genuinely a labour of love, however various may be their opinions, have a common regard for truth. Truth, to them, provides the moral sustenance and a sense of values in the criticism of our time. The substance clapped between the covers of this volume is as politically challenging as it is intellectually stimulating.

I leave you with the incisive commentators and analysts of the towering Radio Cameroon programme: CAMEROON REPORT.

Professor Tatah Mentan has been a visiting scholar of Peace and Security, Global Political Economy and African Studies in several North American Universities – including Concordia University, St Paul Minnesota – for more than a decade. His most recent testamental publications include: *Democracy for Breakfast? Unveiling Mirage Democracy in Contemporary Africa.*

Introduction

It is more than an academic privilege to be called upon to contribute an introduction to a book on "Cameroon Report", a land mark in investigative journalism and a source of hope and inspiration for many a voiceless Cameroonian over the years. Although for long a fan of "Cameroon Report", my first meeting ever with its crew was in 1988 during a fieldwork exercise on the role of the broadcast media in nation-building in Cameroon. I remember suggesting to George Tanni, producer of the programme before its suspension in June 1986, to seriously consider the publication of past contributions to "Cameroon Report". The present collection by Sam-Nuvala Fonkem, long-time member of the "Cameroon Report" team, can only be saluted as a step in that direction.

"Cameroon Report" hardly needs introducing any longer, especially to well-informed Cameroonians of English expression. Started in 1972, "Cameroon Report" rapidly gained in reputation as a mirror of social ills, an inspector-general of public life, and the custodian of national ideals and aspirations. It was hypercritical of government action; never hesitating to point the finger at any one in high office for apparent inefficiency. This inevitably led to its being considered by those in high office as a nuisance, a thorn in their flesh. But for a decade Ahidjo tolerated "Cameroon Report" despite his conformist exigencies on the media. He had come to tolerate "Cameroon Report" as a relevant nuisance, and to use it as a defence against accusations of repression and the lack of freedom of expression.

The spirit of "Cameron Report" was in stark contrast with that of its French equivalent, "Dimanche Midi". The difference in style and approach was unmistakable. "Cameroon Report" journalists claimed to be "Anglo-Saxon" in style, and to be inspired by "investigative reporting". Their interest was and remains to present the facts without comment and let the audience make their own opinions. To them, the public has the right to know the facts, undiluted and unmitigated. The "Dimanche Midi" journalists on the other hand believe in the "Latin" style. Accordingly, they tend to wait for events, they present themselves most of the time as the mouthpiece of the government; all they do is propagate "la bonne parole officielle" by receiving directives from the presidency and the ministries.

It is an irony that "Cameroon Report" survived Ahidjo's dictatorship but could not survive Biya's democracy. For it was at a time of alleged democracy and tolerance, a period when Cameroonians did not have to flee their country or go underground to express their opinions, that "Cameroon Report", a programme much loved and cherished, a nuisance that even Ahidjo had dared to consider relevant, met its denouement. Just how did this happen?

On Friday 20 June 1986, "Cameroon Report" was suspended indefinitely for being a constant embarrassment to the authorities of the New Deal Government. The Minister of Information and Culture at the time, Prof. George Ngango, was questioned in parliament why he allowed "his journalists" to use the airwaves to attack parliamentarians. Angered, he came back and gave instructions for the programme to be suspended. "Cameroon Report" was later substituted by a less critical and more conformist programme "News Panorama"; a substitute which Sam- Nuvala Fonkem described as "a fake... a counterfeit". The "Cameroon Report" team did not like the indefinite suspension of their programme; most of them refused to have anything to do with the "News Panorama".

Meanwhile on June 26 1986, following an event that was not unconnected, three newscasters namely Sam- Nuvala Fonkem, Ebssiy Ngum and Johnny MacViban were arrested and detained for nearly four months in connection with a news talk presented by Sam-Nuvala Fonkem in the English-language evening newscast on Tuesday 24 June 1986, titled "Enemies of Democracy"; a talk which was seen to be critical of certain members of parliament. Finally released, none of the journalists was sent back to broadcasting; instead, Ebssiy Ngum and Johnny MacViban were transferred to *Cameroon Tribune* to work as print journalists, while Sam- Nuvala Fonkem was sent to teach in the Advanced School of Mass Communication (ASMAC/ESSTI).

Neither in the transfers of the three broadcasters nor in the suspension and subsequent replacement of "Cameroon Report" was the opinion of the Cameroonian public sought, let alone that of the broadcasters involved. It is not common for the authorities to seek the opinion of civil servants before transferring them; nor do they sample public opinion of civil servants before transferring them, nor do they sample public opinion often enough. Not surprising therefore, as Sam-Nuvala Fonkem explained, round about 1980/81 Bwele Guillaume, in his capacity as Information and Culture Minister, wanted the schedule of "Cameroon Report" to be changed, not because the public wanted it that way, but because he was used to going jogging on Sunday mornings and therefore did not always have time to monitor the programme.

There is no doubt that "Cameroon Report", right from inception, has always been an embarrassment to those in power. Its poignant honesty did not leave any one in government indifferent. Ahidjo tolerated it more as a fangless bulldog than anything else. Each time the dog threatened to come out with any surprises, it was contained. There were well elaborated administrative control mechanisms for that. These ranged from the overt suppression of information to such sanctions on failure to conform as transfers, interrogations by the police and suspensions.

Thus for example, in 1981 the government, increasingly embarrassed by this self-elected watchdog of the commonwealth in the name of "Cameroon Report", transferred the programme's key members from Yaounde, the National Station, to the provincial stations. In the same transfer decree Julius Wamey was transferred to Radio Bamenda, Victor Epie Ngome to Radio Douala, Asonglefac Nkemleke to Buea, and Akwanka Joe Ndifor to Bafoussam. However, this particular transfer failed to "kill" the programme, because "the authorities made the error of dealing with individuals" rather than with "the spirit", with the result that George Tanni and the other broadcasters who were brought to replace transferred colleagues, continued in the same vein, even receiving contributions from them in the provinces. In the words of Sam- Nuvala Fonkem, "you can kill a man, but you don't kill ideas".

"Cameroon Report was silenced but the spirit lived on. Elsewhere on television, a programme, "Minute by Minute" was started and conducted very much along the lines of "Cameroon Report". Akwanka Joe Ndifor, its producer, agrees that his idea was to deliver on screen what had been stifled on radio. Naturally, "Minute by Minute" made many a member of government see Akwanka as a veritable thorn in their hypersensitive flesh. It too was killed eventually, but not before some historic experiences of its own.

Akwanka Joe Ndifor recounted how the former Minister of Industry and Commerce, Edward Nomo Ongolo, threatened him for repeatedly showing a programme in which the Minister had blundered immensely. Interviewed for the programme "Minute by Minute", the Minister had defended the importation of rice with the claim that foreign rice was four times easier to cook than Cameroonian rice. Seeing this as a grave misjudgement from a member of a government with a policy of self-reliant development, Akwanka criticised the Minister on TV; a thing the latter was not ready to stomach. He threatened "to kill" Akwanka, but lost his post before he could do so. Earlier, in 1985, still at the time of "Cameroon Report", Sam-Nuvala Fonkem had been threatened with dismissal, imprisonment and death, because of a contribution he made to the programme, 18/8/1989, titled "Harmonising Our Two Legal Systems". A drama which ended in the dismissal of the Minister of Justice and Keeper of the Seals, Ngongang Ouandji and the Minister of Information and Culture, François Sengat Kuo.

The struggle of "Cameroon Report" and the media as a whole over the years to establish a fourth estate was met with undue and unreasonable resistance on the part of the central authorities. This notwithstanding, the tested persistence of the spirit of "Cameroon Report" ought to serve as an inspiration to every media practitioner in an oppressed system.

Francis B. Nyamnjoh, Professor of Social Anthropology, University of Cape Town, South Africa

Editor's Note

This collection has been aptly described as the 'Voices of Dissent' and comes in a timely manner to dispel the widespread impression that the official media have been indifferent with regard to the struggle for human rights and the freedom of expression.

Granted that the official media in Cameroon were swiftly transformed into an instrument of blatant propaganda and disinformation in the wake of the public outcry for open democracy in the 1990s, nevertheless, the weekly English language program of the National Service of Radio Cameroon, Cameroon Report (now Cameroon Calling) has always been at the forefront of the campaign for freedoms since its inception in 1972.

The authoritative, objective, critical and prophetic nature of the selections in this collection is evidence that press freedom is never served on a silver platter but must be wrested from the iron hands of despotism.

In compiling this collection, it was not possible to lay hands on material broadcast before 1978 as the early producers paid little attention to documentation. A considerable amount of this material was furnished from the private archives of the commentators and analysts while the rest was made after a minute selection from some 1.000 articles that survived and were salvaged from the drawers of the English Desk by the Editor.

A number of factors such as the magnitude of events and prominence of people, overall government policy, and issues of vital human interest determined the choice of articles in this collection.

Cameroon Report, which has undergone two name changes since 1986 (News Panorama and now Cameroon Calling) was initially conceived in 1972 as a radio newsreel on events of the week but gradually evolved into a definitive program of critical news analysis and commentary whose concern for the welfare of society and whose commitment to the promotion of freedom of expression and social responsibility in the true sense of the word have gone a long way to elevate Cameroon Journalism.

Apart from articles which came in Cameroon Report proper some news talks have been included to give this collection a wider dimension.

The anthology is divided into two sections: domestic and foreign issues and events with articles arranged chronologically to facilitate a grasp of the historical evolution of events and ideas.

Editing basically was directed at rendering these articles in print form and no attempt has been made to modify their original content and flavour. Care was also taken to preserve the style of the spoken language as these materials were conceived and written for broadcast.

The dates mentioned at the top of each article could either be the date it was written or the date of broadcast. So many years have gone by and it is quite a task to determine the exact dates of broadcast.

Rather than use the footnote approach, supplementary information was incorporated in a great number of the introductions to the commentaries to help readers situate issues and events. Where original introductions were completely absent, editing took care of that.

In short, what the editor has done is mere selection and packaging and lays no claim to any accomplishment beyond that.

The Prologue

The significance of this collection can only be appreciated if readers bear in mind that the socio-political context in which journalists and especially those of the official media operated in the 1970s and 80s was marked by an authoritarian communication model that was implemented through the application of censorship i.e. prior restraint for the private press and self censorship for the state-owned media manned by inflexible gatekeepers who were committed to the concept of highly centralised government and the one-party political ideology.

The notion of pluralism or respect for diversity of opinion was very remote. Even President Biya who incarnated a certain measure of hope for a more liberal dispensation when he just took over power from the "Father of the Nation" Ahmadou Ahidjo in 1982 reminded his countrymen that: "Truth comes from above and rumours from below."

Private newspapers which could be counted on one's finger tips had to submit dummies of every edition of the paper to the local administrative authority who took all their sweet time to run their red pens over the work, cancelling anything they perceived as unfavourable to government image before putting their stamp of approval. At times entire editions were simply censored.

At the level of the state-owned media i.e. the national daily newspaper "Cameroon Tribune" and Radio Cameroon and the audio-visual media, control was ensured through the careful choice of gatekeepers or managers, editors appointed by Presidential and Ministerial decree while journalists were recruited mainly from the state-run professional schools and educational establishments.

It was understood that products of such schools had been sufficiently groomed to toe the official line because right from the moment of admission into school after a competitive examination, one was invariably considered a state employee in the making. Output was closely monitored by supervisors and managers who were keen on spotting out any deviations from the editorial line. For example news relating coups d'état or coup plots, separatist movements and human rights violations were taboo and needed clearance from the editors who themselves needed clearance from the hierarchy.

While this was the case, the Ahidjo and Biya regimes, especially Ahidjo, recognised that in spite of their marginalised status in the scheme of things, the Anglophones had what we can simply call the Anglo-Saxon character; a character marked by a remarkable penchant for accountability, open debate and outspokenness- a legacy of its British-derived parliamentary system inculcated when Anglophone Cameroon (Southern Cameroons) was administered by Britain as a League of Nations Mandated territory (1922- 1945) and subsequently as a UN Trust Territory. The Southern Cameroons, in a bid to assert its self determination, had petitioned and obtained from Britain its own separate parliament from Nigeria through which it was administered for administrative expedience in 1953. This was long before France granted to French Cameroon a teleguided territorial assembly in 1957.

President Ahidjo, unlike Biya, was known for paying attention to alternative and informal sources of information apart from the official sources including the dreaded political police CENER aka CEDOC aka DIRDOC. He accommodated Cameroon Report as a credible source of public opinion which official sources took care to conceal from him. Sometime around 1978 or '79, I was unable to get to the Radio House early enough one Sunday morning to present the programme which came up at 7a.m. This caused quite a stir and by mid-day envoys had been sent to fetch me to go and present the programme. On failing to hear the programme that morning, the Big Man had called the Minister who being a late sleeper had not noticed the non broadcast of CR. The said Minister later tried to get the CR team to change the broadcast time to no avail. After this incident, it became clear to the barons of the regime that CR was not to be toyed with because the Old Man himself was a fan of the programme.

Despite its reputation for outspokenness, the CR team had to tread with caution. The keen reader would get a sense of self censorship when he comes across quite a few articles like the one dealing with the admission into the OAU of the nationalist movement, the Polisario Front that had declared the separation of the Western Sahara from Morocco's tutelage; a question that had split the OAU.

The government position was pro Morocco but deep down the hearts of the CR crew, our sympathy was for the Polisario Front as it had always been for the underdog, but this time we had no choice but to toe the official line. Every time the government took a clear position on a major issue, we had to toe the line.

In cases where the government had not come out clearly with a position, we took liberties such as supporting the pro-Soviet/Cuba MPLA nationalist movement in Angola to the utter discomfort of the regime which was perceived to be pro-French, hence pro-Western as well as our unflattering opinion of French "coopérants".

We took risks and played with the devil's tail but we were inoculated by our "Anglophoneness". Perhaps it can be argued that Ahidjo tolerated CR because of its small Anglophone audience at home and the liberal image it gave of Cameroon to an international audience; a good international PR gimmick, so to speak. He could use CR to counter any detractor who accused Cameroon of disregarding freedom of expression.

Paul Biya who succeeded Ahidjo in 1982 very much let CR alone. He had declared from the outset that he wanted to be remembered as the one who brought democracy to Cameroon and CR like all other organs of the private and state media at the dawn of his accession to power gave him unflinching support during the row that developed between him and Ahidjo over the latter's plans to perpetuate his control of the state. Ahidjo was about to cause the adoption of constitutional reforms that would consecrate the supremacy of the CNU party- of which he was still Chairman- over the state; a ploy that would allow him run the state by remote control even though he had resigned as President of the republic. Unfortunately this collection does not have the series of commentaries backing the pro-Biya legalistic arguments.

The Ahidjo-Biya row culminated in the 6 April 1984 coup attempt by forces loyal to Ahidjo. Biya enjoyed enormous support from the press. However it is worth recalling that for the first time, all commentaries in the aftermath of the coup attempt including all CR articles underwent prior censorship with the Minister of Information, Sengat Kuo himself playing the chief censor. I recall that I had concluded my paper with the observation that in order to avoid public antipathy, any future constitutional reform should consider putting term limitations on presidential mandates as this was one of the major reasons for disgruntlement with the Ahidjo regime that had lasted 24 years in power. Sengat Kuo deleted that last paragraph.

Despite the anxiousness of the new regime's gatekeepers to ensure conformity and compliance, a new dynamism that come with every peaceful political transition could be felt among media practitioners both in the public and private sectors. We at Cameroon Report dug our feet into the little opening to ensure the door did not suddenly close on us after coming this far. We were emboldened to question things we might have been too cautious to question before. One of us, Eric Chinje, captured the mood in his commentary titled: "The task ahead for President Paul Biya" broadcast a day after the man's inaugural on 6 November 1982. "The excitement is over, and the euphoria must make way for some cool and level headed thinking. Some hard questions, some difficult answers! Independence, reunification, unification, peace, stability and progress," he declared. In order words, it was time to start critically examining certain notions everyone had so far been taking for granted. He continued: "...popular concerns among the majority of this programme, Cameroon Report's national audience. There are obvious questions about the places that English and French continue to occupy in the national linguistic package." Eric was speaking not only on behalf of Cameroon Report but on behalf of Anglophone Cameroonians (CR's national audience) who were being treated as second class citizens. The marginalisation of the Anglophone and his territory which was the source of the nation's wealth (crude oil, the vast CDC oil palm, rubber, tea and banana plantations and the oil refinery –SONARA) became a crusade for CR thereafter. Hear Eric: "On the question of regional development, will the mould of stagnation, decay and neglect that hangs over once vibrant urban communities as Limbe, Kumba, Mamfe, and Bamenda dissipate? Will the man in Fako feel even more a part of the SONARA reality than he has been wont to feel?"

Given the benefit of hindsight, we can better appreciate the weight of the concerns expressed in 1982 when we realise that 31 years later, one can still count on his finger tips the number of Anglophones in SONARA which had become a mafia of the Bassa ethnic group until a new GM from the north was recently (2013) appointed but which does not and will not change the regional equation. SONARA still pays its taxes to the Douala Treasury in French-speaking Cameroon and not in Limbe where it is located.

We raised issues hitherto considered taboo. We castigated the wasteful and corrupt management of public corporations, the irksome ordeal of citizens and civil servants flocking to Yaoundé to 'chase' administrative files, we questioned the raison d'être of the wasteful two-shifts working day which the Francophones loved so much because they could go home to a copious lunch and wine after which they kissed the second shift to hell. Getting the regime to change to the one shift system (which the Francophones resisted because it was what obtained in the Anglophone part of the country) was one of the few battles we won.

We had also become increasingly vocal about the lip service paid to the policy of bilingualism manifested by the unapologetic snobbery of the English language by the Francophone ruling class including its Anglophone quisling proxies who felt obliged to conduct government business only in French. As recently as 2012, the Chairman of the INTELCAM the telecommunications corporation, Honourable, Chief Victor E. Mukete, octogenarian and one of the early proponents of unification, openly complained about the exclusive use of French in a telecommunications conference he was chairing in Yaoundé and how every working document was only in French. Over centralised government, regional imbalance in development, poor health delivery system and neglect of the peasant farmer were among some of the targets of our crusade.

The Anglophone/Francophone dichotomy was quite visible in the legal systems operating in Cameroon. Differences in the two criminal procedures: the Francophone, marked by civil law and the inquisitorial philosophy whereby the accused was guilty until s/he proves otherwise and the Anglophone Common law –derived system, marked by the accusatorial approach whereby the accused is presumed innocent until proven guilty beyond reasonable doubt by the court and the respect for habeas corpus and due process continued to be a major source of clashes, misunderstanding, frustrations and bitterness between the judicial hierarchy and the Anglophone magisterial corps.

Sometime in 1985, an Anglohone State Counsel (public prosecutor) of Limbe, Mr. Metuge I believe, had ordered the arrest of the GM of SONARA, Bernard Eding on allegations of oil bunkering involving a Spanish boat from Equatorial Guinea that had anchored off the Limbe West Coast and was clandestinely loading refined petroleum from the SONARA refinery. In typical fashion, the Francophone gendarme who had been sent to execute the warrant of arrest, preferred to negotiate a juicy, some say CFA 5 million francs, deal that allowed Eding to escape to his Yaoundé masters. While in

Limbe on a personal trip, I met Mr. Metuge by chance and he furnished me with a copy of the charge file against Eding who had now mobilised the Minister of Justice and other big guns in Yaoundé to harass poor Metuge. I kept the copy of the file which I could not immediately exploit for Cameroon Report for obvious reasons until one fine day after the Minister of Justice had ended a tour of the North-West and South-West provinces to castigate Anglophone magistrates for "ignorance of judicial procedures" etc. The last but one commentary in this collection: "Harmonising the Two legal Systems" deals with this issue and earned me an administrative query that was just the beginning of a disciplinary procedure that could jolly well end in several unpleasant possibilities including a sack from the radio, indefinite suspension or a delay in career advancement. The Minister of Justice, Ngongang Ouandji and the Governor of the South-West province Maggloire Nguiamba had written to the Minister of Information Sengat Kuo and copied the Minister of Territorial Administration (Interior) to take severe disciplinary action against me for daring to even speak about such a very delicate matter concerning the Eding case file and for taking sides with Anglophone magistrates. This was by far the closest brush I was having with the high authorities and several of them at one go.

By the time the sledge hammer was about to land on my head, a miracle happened. One fine Saturday afternoon- the 1.30 pm newscast had been delayed for more than an hour- a surprise cabinet reshuffle was read over Radio Yaounde. All three heavy weights: Ministers of Justice, Information and Territorial Administration were sacked! Coincidence? An act of God? Could the Minister of Justice have truly burnt his fingers over the Eding matter? The answer is blowing in the wind.

After this incident, CR began treading on slippery grounds. It began stepping on some toes and some high-ups were becoming uncomfortable. On one fateful Friday, 20 June I guess, we had variously strolled into the newsroom at different times and were taken aback by a hand-written note stuck on the notice board asking the CR crew to suspend production until further notice. I had come into the newsroom to start extracting a "feed" for CR from a long interview I had conducted during the week with Barrister Ben Muna, newly- elected President (Batonier) of the Cameroon Bar Council.

We quickly rallied every member of the crew for an emergency meeting during which we learnt that a certain Member of Parliament, Lobe Nwalipenja of Ndian division had sometime after the March 1986 CPDM local party elections in which he lost to a retired policemen-a political novice- had complained bitterly about the way CR had handled his defeat. These elections, the first of its kind, were some kind of an early experiment in democracy Biya was trying to carry out at the level of the one party system to test the true popularity of the party leaders. Whether Biya intended by this to indicate an eventual return to multiparty politics is very doubtful. Mr. Nwalipenja was still smarting from his defeat when the Minister of Information appeared before the Finance Committee of the National Assembly (of which he was a member) budgetary session in June to vent his anger at him: Are you asking this Committee for an increase in budgetary allocations to give your journalists to insult us, he is believed to have queried the Minister.

At the emergency meeting of the crew, it was agreed that even though CR had been suspended indefinitely, we had not been expressly banned from making news talks. We were going to take advantage of this loophole to regain our voice. A plan was quickly drawn up with topics freely chosen and a timetable to present a news talk each at the end of the evening newscast. George Tanni, head of the English-language news desk had to begin the following Monday. Meanwhile in place of CR on Sunday morning, CR anchor Ebssiy Ngum contented himself with the reading of an epitaph announcing the death of CR.

Come Monday and George reneged. He suddenly developed cold feet. When my turn came on Tuesday, I had a difficult choice to make: chicken out or take the bull by the horn and preserve the tradition we had all stood for. I knew I wrote more than a dozen drafts in the newsroom that Tuesday evening and none seemed potent enough to convey our exasperation with this new kind of censorship instigated by a politician whom we considered had lost his legitimacy. To spare the readers all the details and cut a long story short, what was delivered when I entered the studio at the tail end of the news was an extempore performance that was more potent for its tone than its words,; it was a jerky, unrehearsed and emotionally charged indictment of what became known in Cameroon as "monkeys and hand clappers". That commentary, so to speak, was the funeral oration for CR as it once was.

Some five years later, a new political dispensation, marked by the restoration of multipartism that had been killed in September 1966 with the formation of the Cameroon National Union (CNU) as the sole political party, was ushered in. It came with its own ramifications, trials and tribulations for media practitioners; it came with its own frustrations, hopes and disappointments. It ushered in a vibrant private press as newspapers mushroomed on newspaper kiosks throughout the main urban centres. We shall have a taste of that vibrancy in a separate collection titled SNAPSHOT a compilation of personal analyses and commentaries published in the private press between 1991 and 2008; a reflection of the political aspirations of the time.

1

Cameroon Report 1/9/78: The C.N.U: Twelve Years After

Introduction: *Today marks one dozen years in the life of the Cameroon National Union party – the CNU. At birth on September 1, 1966, the CNU was saddled with the outwardly impressive responsibility of building and preserving national unity, truth, and democracy in Cameroon. News commentator Tatah Mentan has these observations:*

From all indications, the unity, truth and democracy have not thrived in a straight and steady path, nor in direct proportion to the efforts of its high priests. The dirty fingers of Cameroonian economic, political and social reality boldly mark the ivory walls of creeds.

On such an occasion, therefore, it would be morally wrong for a concerned Cameroonian journalist to become a mere-pen-pusher to the great in his society or to pander to the mighty. He must address the issues at stake sincerely and humbly knowing that the collective efforts of Cameroonians can always move them closer to the angels.

First of all, the goal of national unity is nowhere in sight. One often gathers the impression that it is a mere disguise to split a section of the country into provinces and thrust against another section whose territorial and political unity has jealously been fostered. This policy should gratefully be abandoned as a tissue of contradictions and confusion if the so-called national unity is to mean more than a pipe-dream at best and the nursing of a civil war at worst.

Secondly, the quest for truth within the CNU has been replaced by accusations of social irresponsibility and greed by renewed appeals to patriotism and other political spirits and by a mood of growing pessimism and despair. The reason is that the path has been so privatized that truth has been sacrificed on the altar of saying only what the Chairman wants to hear. Truth cannot flower in an atmosphere of conformity too thick to nurture democracy.

Thirdly, the bulldog confidence in democracy in the Cameroonian society has evaporated. Democracy in Cameroon has become shop-talk with no end but itself. Funny enough, there is no government on earth which hesitates to label itself prestigiously as democratic. IDI AMIN's Uganda, BOTHA's South Africa, PINOCHET's Chile and what have you, claim the mantle of democracy. This is an abusive use of the word *democracy*. Common sense tells us that democracy compels choice on the electorate, imposes public accountability on the authorities, confers fundamental human rights on the populace, etc. A national torture chamber can thus never be a democratic place.

These sad and shocking experiences do not mean that all hopes are lost. One way of redeeming the uncomfortable situation is by appreciating the critical truth that whatever or whoever makes peaceful change impossible makes violent change inevitable.

Finally, intelligent and free discussion is normally the primary basis for attaining the ultimate goal of social perfectibility. In Cameroon, national unity, truth, and democracy thirst after this ultimate goal of social perfectibility.

Tatah Mentan

2

Cameroon Report 18/1/81: Wum Farmer-Grazier Problem

Introduction: *The perennial farmer-grazier problem has once again reared its ugly head. Our specialist, Wilfred Nkwenti has this analysis:*

The civil disturbance in Wum, capital of Menchum Division, in the North West Province, which resulted in loss of life, several wounded and loss of property early this month, has come to confirm the fragility of providing only temporary solutions to urgent human problems, while postponing the quest for more permanent solutions to future instances.

It is an example of what could happen when those concerned remain insensitive or indifferent, even if only partially, to a people's cry. The first real sign of a serious problem between the cattle- rearing Mbororo-Fulani people and the native peasant farmers of Aghem, Wum, manifested itself in 1973. That year, Aghem tribeswomen marched on to Bamenda to protest against the destruction of their crops by cattle let free by the Fulani graziers.

We are informed that the provincial administration went down to Wum and set aside specific areas of land for cattle grazing and others for farming. Similar arrangements have been made in other parts of the North West Province with similar problems. But such a solution has everywhere proved itself inadequate and evidence of this is the many violations of farmer/grazer boundaries, and in most by the grazers through whose negligence their cattle stray into neighbouring farms, causing lamentable destruction to growing crops which constitute the only hope for existence of many peasant families. There have also been cases of peasant families going to farm in rich valleys, ironically set aside as cattle grazing land.

Since, perhaps, the last one quarter century, there have been thousands of quarrels between farmers and cattle rearers in the North West Province.

There is constant agitation by the native farmers because while the population grows and intensifies the pressure for farm land, the land itself, especially the available arable land, is not inelastic.

The agitation has mostly come from the farmers because they bear the brunt of many problems between themselves and the cattle. In the first place, crops do not move from the farms to the cattle. It is the cattle that move. Crops do not destroy cattle whereas one cow alone can bring whole families to the brink of famine for a whole season. Thirdly, the farmers, poor as they are, do not attract the same sympathy as the rich cattle rearers who can "play up" in the event of a quarrel between the two.

What puzzles anyone of good faith is, why had the situation in Wum which had showed itself to be grave as far back as 1973 to deteriorate seemingly unnoticed or simply unattended, to the lamentable incident of January 1, 1981 which cost human life or limb and property?

Without attempting to insinuate that the persistence of farmer/grazer problems benefit some selfish, unpatriotic enemies of peace, it is to be hoped that a just and lasting solution will henceforth be found, consequent upon the Wum incident, not only for the farmer/grazier problems in

Cameroon, but for any urgent human problem that is perceived.

Wilfred Nkwenti

3

Cameroon Report 28/3/1982: A chaotic Highway Transporters Union

Introduction: *This week, representatives of the Cameroon Highway Transporters Union, SETRACAUCAM, held their 4th national congress in Yaounde with proposed increases of transport fares high on the agenda. SAM-NUVALA FONKEM examines road transport in this country and condemns what he sees as the indifference of union workers to the plight of travellers and the absence of any decent facilities in motor-parks:*

There are unmistakable signs that the transport union, Setracaucam, is headed for increases in transport fares and that figures yet to be published show a hike of about 17%. Whether these increases are justified or not is not the question. Granted that such increases fall within the framework of government policy to adjust prices in various economic sectors to create a balance and foster social justice, what the public is concerned about is whether the union is prepared to take concrete measures to ensure that official transport fares are respected by park-collectors.

Past observations clearly show that passengers are made to pay higher fares than the official rates despite empty assurances by union leaders. Before suggesting what measure should be taken to safeguard the interest of the public, this reporter could like to take leave to examine certain claims of improvement in the organisation of road transport made by the president of the union.

Although the president of the union acknowledged certain discrepancies in the handling of passenger's luggage, reckless driving and illegal increases in transport fares, he did not say in what ways the union intends to resolve these discrepancies. The union president mentioned the existence of certain facilities in motor-parks which we have reason to question, such as waiting rooms and storage for baggage. He also cited as one of the union's achievements, a greater sense of civic responsibility on the part of the park-collectors and bus drivers.

Apparently, Mr. Union President has never visited a motor-park, at least, as an ordinary observer, since, as a union executive, he obviously travels 1st class by Cameroon Airlines. This reporter would like to challenge Mr. Union President to roll-up his trousers, take off his executive tie and visit the parks before making claims of a better organisation of road transport. He forgot to mention the continued extortion of arbitrary charges for excess baggage because the long-promised use of scales in motor-parks has never materialized.

Mr. Union President informs us that one of the achievements of the union within the past five years is the existence of food-stands in motor-parks, but he did not seem to see any sanitation related problems in these food-stands which are run by independent hawkers who seem not to be bound by any health regulation. He also referred to the filthy shacks erected with metal scraps and cardboard which he calls waiting rooms for passengers as an achievement. Although he stressed that the union has improved on the civic education of its workers, the union president overlooked the shabby treatment of passengers by filthy, rude and uncouth park-collectors who do not hesitate to rough-handle passengers and baggage alike.

The union leader may not also be aware that during the rainy seasons when passengers have to push the vehicle through long stretches of mud, women and girls are denied the right to travel, a discrimination based on sex which is against the spirit of our legislation.

Looking at the catalogue of so-called achievements, one agrees that the union has a long way to go in terms of building all-weather motor-parks, the respect of the Highway Code, the attitude of union workers towards their travellers and the setting up of more congenial refreshment facilities and public conveniences. First and foremost, the union must set up a mechanism to ensure that passengers' rights and official transport fares are respected.

Most of the immoral activities of the union are perpetuated by the fact that the consumer is helpless and has no forum for seeking redress.

This reporter is suggesting the setting up of an independent complaints bureau with an ombudsman appointed by the Ministry of Economic Affairs and Planning since they are a partner to the price fixing mechanism, to ensure that motor-parks operate within the limits of regulations governing their operation.

This appears to be the only concrete and surest mechanism to lend any credibility and confidence to the highway transporters union whose emergence has rather brought about more anarchy, corruption and disrespect in the road transport business than there was before its creation.

Sam-Nuvala Fonkem

4

Cameroon Report 5/4/81: Inhuman prison conditions

Introduction: *Very recently, the Minister of State and the Vice Minister of Territorial Administration visited the prisons in Yaounde and Douala and came up with astounding revelations about the inadequacy of penitentiary institutions, the delay in the execution of legal procedures concerning detainees and the general inhuman conditions in which prisoners live. ADAMU MUSA has this grim survey of our prisons system:*

There are two thousand persons detained in the Douala Central prison. On construction, the capacity of this prison was meant to take five hundred persons. Recent modifications increased the capacity to eight hundred.

The case in the Yaounde Central Prison is even more awful. There are two thousand, two hundred detainees with groups of one hundred crammed into cells meant for twenty-five persons. The situation in other prisons all over the country is certainly not very different. Think of the unpleasant heat in these two cities where one is not even at case in well ventilated houses. And then imaging the hell fire in which these prisoners live, knowing well that prison cells are hardly ever ventilated.

There are cases where cholera epidemics are known to have broken out in the Douala Central prison, and prisoners are known to have committed suicide in the Yaounde Central prison just because of the extremely uncomfortable and inhuman conditions in which they happen to live.

The death rate in those prisons is also known to have risen sharply. The very horrible prison conditions lead one to ask the question whether prisons are meant to serve as a punitive domain for the unfortunate ones whose crimes, through some miscalculation, happened to have been exposed. Imprisonment is supposed to serve both as a punitive measure and as an opportunity for the delinquent to mediate on his crime so as to change for good once his liberty is restored.

Imprisonment is also supposed to serve as a forum wherein the delinquent is educated on his responsibilities as a citizen and on his behaviour as a social being. These deplorable conditions in which our delinquent citizens are made to live do not help them in any way. On the contrary, the lucky few who survive the ordeal to the end become more hardened when they finally regain their freedom.

In our over-crowded prisons are found criminals of all categories, ages and backgrounds. No wonder then that our prisons serve as a school where more crimes are learnt by the somewhat milder inmates. In an interview given to Cameroon Tribune on March 14 this year, the most senior boss of prisons administration disclosed that he discovered that prisoners took knives and Indian hemp into their cells and that dangerous fights were common amongst them. Not everyone who goes to prison is necessarily a criminal. But God alone, or more fittingly, the devil alone knows better what threat these people pose to society on their release.

I know there used to be a time in the English-speaking part of this country when one went to prison, he learnt some trade say carpentry, brick laying, and what have you? On return to civilian life, these persons never felt out of place for they could at least earn a living. And then the threats the ex-convicts of today are posing to society were virtually non-existent. But alas! gone are those days and here we are with crime and insecurity growing by leaps and bounds for the devil continues to find work for idle hands.

One reason for the over-crowding in our prisons which has led to the appalling sanitary and feeding conditions is that there are far more people just awaiting trial than those actually condemned.

There are embarrassingly painful instances where people are known to have been awaiting trial for more than five years and nobody just seems to care about them. Then, on some lucky day, their case files happen to find their way to court and they are either discharged and acquitted or sentenced for say six months. But then they would have already spent five years or more in prison. Situations like these are not only due to the fact that our judges have many cases that they cannot handle within record time as it is claimed. I would believe, in a large measure, it is due to the paradoxical legal interpretation that an accused person is guilty and consequently a prisoner until he proves the contrary.

Well, if the delay in the examination of cases is due to a shortage of magistrates, the solution is easy because there are hundreds of graduates in law roaming our streets today without any jobs. Nobody is asking that a paradise be created for delinquents. God forbid that.

One is only concerned about these developments because one does not need to be omniscient to know that a large percentage of us in this country are potential prisoners, and are only fortunate to stay out because we may have the trump cards in our hands and could manipulate them the way we want. Good enough, the Minister of State in charge of Territorial Administration and his assistant have openly shown their dissatisfaction with the conditions reigning in our prisons and have promised that something is being done to ameliorate the living conditions of these unfortunate citizens for a better re-integration into society when they regain their liberty. We hope something is done about it soon.

Adamu Musa

5

Cameroon Report 5/4/1981: Lay Private Education

Introduction: *The General Assembly of the Organization of Lay Private Education was held in Yaounde this week to discuss the status of private educational schools and the inadequacy and modalities for the award of government grants-in-aid. AKWANKA JOE NDIFOR examines the deplorable conditions of teaching and learning in lay private educational institutions and suggests that government ensure the effective use of grants to these institutions:*

The first duty of every government is to guarantee the education, health and security of its citizens. The government of this country has given priority to the education of our citizens. That is why the Ministry of Education has the largest budget. We all agree that it is impossible for the government to own all the schools alone. That is why it encourages individuals to open private schools under official auspices – schools officially known as lay private educational institutions.

Most parents have described the proprietors of lay private schools as thieves or rogues who are out to steal their money under the guise of education of the leaders of tomorrow's Cameroon. Intensive research has proved that parents are not far from the truth.

A close look at lay private schools reveals that most of them are run under the most deplorable conditions. The goal of any school is to obtain good results in official examinations. But the greed of proprietors to make a fortune for themselves has thrown this goal far into the background.

The Propaganda nature of the names of these schools is fascinating. Proprietors choose names which very often lead to tautology to give the impression that the schools are comprehensive whereas only one form of education is offered. The result is arbitrary raises in school fees to incredible amounts.

The laxity in discipline has become so pronounced that most people describe these establishments as brothels for breeding harlots. Proprietors most often present fake statistics to evade government taxes and get more subventions.

Accommodation for students has degenerated so that today students live in squalor and acute congestion. Feeding is a disgrace. The staff is dominated by unqualified teachers. The result is very poor performances in official examinations.

The conditions under which teachers work in lay private schools are a major contributing factor to this output. Very often, there are delays in the payment of teacher's salaries. At times salaries are confiscated because the proprietors claim they have overheard that the teacher plans to go for further studies. Some of these teachers are wrongly categorized. There are no accommodation facilities. Because teachers are few with a corresponding rise in the student population, teachers are heavily over worked – some with a forty-four-hour week. Very often, proprietors humiliate teachers in front of students.

Proprietors have their complaints also: delays in the payment of school fees, rising costs, inadequate government subventions and the untimely departure of teachers. It is because of these schools. But then, we begin to question the seriousness of the government in the education of young Cameroonians. The government has so far failed to ensure the effective use of subventions and the right to make laws for lay private schools. Lay schools handle more than 3/4 of the student population. But they receive only 20% of government subventions.

The disparity in teacher's salaries between the private and the public sectors is so wide that there is the tendency for teachers to drift from the private to the public sector.

It has also been observed that the provincial delegations of education have become dumping grounds for qualified teachers whereas they are lacking in the private sector. Provincial Education Commissions are utterly ineffective because they meet only twice annually.

Scholarships to lay schools are almost nonexistent. The time has come for the government to take austere measures to curb the vice in lay schools such as the setting up of a school fee board to collect fees. The government could send qualified teachers to the private sector and stop the award of subventions.

Provincial commissions should have permanent offices to monitor the day to day activities of these schools. If a school still doesn't improve, then it should be closed down.

Akwanka Joe Ndifor

6

Cameroon Report 5/4/1981: Health for all by year 2000

Introduction: *Cameroon joined the rest of the international community last Tuesday to observe the 33rd World Health Day which centred on the theme, "Health for all by the year 2000." Here in Cameroon, observers are preoccupied with the possibility of achieving such an ambitious goal. Of course, it is possible to achieve health for all by year 2000 or even the year 3000, but looking at the present unequal availability of and accessibility to health care facilities for every citizen, AKWANKA JOE NDIFOR remarks that it is rather ironical that health care is provided free to those who can afford it while the poverty-stricken masses are deprived of it:*

How far is it possible that the health of every Cameroonian shall be guaranteed by the year 2000? Cameroon Report has no intention of looking at this assertion from a negative perspective. But just as it is normal to ask questions, we must also understand that saying something is one thing and doing it, an entirely different thing.

And talking about doing things, we are all conscious of the fact that the government is, at least, aware of the need to maintain the health of eight million Cameroonians.

This is demonstrated by the fact that the Ministry of Health has the third largest budget in this country. Through this, government has made a fair attempt to establish rural health centres. Pro-pharmacies have been attached to these health centres which sell drugs at reduced prices.

We all agree that it is not yet possible for the government to establish free medical care for every citizen. Perhaps this will come one day. But, when we look at the operation of major health institutions in this country, we begin to cast doubts on the validity of the statement of health for everyone by the year 2000.

Time and time again Cameroon Report has proved that the government-owned hospitals in our big towns are such a humiliation to humanity that some sceptics have ironically described the health ministry as the ministry of death. There is also this question of availability of and accessibility to medical facilities in this country.

The government provides drugs to hospital pharmacies. The destination of these drugs is no longer a mystery because Cameroon Report has observed that these drugs are either diverted to private pharmacies in town where they are sold at cut throat prices or are given free to those who actually stand in a position to purchase them. No doubt the easiest drugs to get from our hospitals are out of stock. Therefore the poor must die because there is no money to buy drugs, although everyone will be healthy by the year 2000.

Many questions have been raised about drug trafficking between government and private pharmacies. There are simple drugs which need no prescriptions to buy but this is not the case because of the absence of patent medicine stores in big urban areas and doctor's prescriptions for drugs to be bought at particular pharmacies.

Most often, dozens of expired drugs in government pharmacies are burnt, thus raising the question of whether these drugs were supposed to be used to treat patients or stored up to be burnt because of the lack of black market customers to buy them.

Still talking about the plight of the poor patient, there is this question of consultation fees. How justified is it that a patient must pay to consult a doctor who is paid by the government? What are the consequences if the patient hasn't the money to pay? A common sight in our towns today is the presence of vagrant mad people, lepers, and other handicapped people – a factor constituting a national disgrace. The situation has remained unchanged over the decades.

The year 2000 is just under two decades from now. The assertion of health for everyone by the year 2000 is a great challenge to our health system which needs a complete overhaul.

Health education must be stepped up to a large extent. The government must ensure that those responsible for the distribution of drugs to the needy be honest citizens who will channel these drugs to the desired destinations.

There is the need for the extension and modernisation of equipment in hospital establishments. Medical doctors are paid by the government. If they have the wish to become private practitioners, then they should be expelled from the Public Service.

The handicapped on our streets are not stronger than the law. Therefore they must disappear into rehabilitation centres. It is only with these that we can dream to attain the objective of the year 2000 and it is only then that critics will no longer refer to the health ministry as the ministry of death.

Akwanka Joe Ndifor

7

Cameroon Report 22/11/81: Catering for disabled persons

Introduction: *Last Friday, the First Lady GERMAINE AHIDJO opened an exhibition of handicraft produced by disabled persons to mark the International Year of Disabled People, IYDP. Society tends to ignore the disabled and generally shows an attitude of intolerance towards them, forgetting that they too are human and can contribute to national development. Activities to mark the IYDP are aimed at drawing public attention on the plight of disabled persons and in the following commentary, MARK NIBOH examines the obligations of the society towards disabled persons and calls for a change of attitude towards them.*

Millions of people are disabled in the world today. In every country, at least one person in ten is disabled by physical, mental or sensory impairment. Yet even these figures do not tell the whole story, for disability is a family affair and affects vast numbers of people who are not themselves disabled. If one member is disabled then the family as a whole is involved in the problems of disability.

Any society which fails to respond effectively to these problems accepts a huge loss of human resources. The promotion of full public awareness of the problems of the disabled and of their right to social equality is very important. Any country with resources to waste should think about the plight of disabled people in the poorest countries. We live in a world of shocking disparities in wealth, literacy, health, opportunity, life expectancy and hope. And we will never have a really safe and stable world while we have the gross and glaring inequalities which so divide and disfigure the world today.

The problem of disabled people is not only one of resources but of political will and priority. That is why we must praise the Cameroon government's efforts in running institutions like the National Rehabilitation Centre for Disabled persons at Etoug Ebe in Yaounde. Praise also goes to other missionary and privately run institutions. We encourage them to go ahead and even improve on the present situation. We must try to improve public attitudes towards the disabled. For centuries, disabled people have been regarded as outcasts in the society, due to fear based on ignorance and misinformation.

Massive public awareness campaigns must be aimed at helping non-disabled people to see that it is often their negative attitudes that the disabled find hardest to bear. Such campaigns must also stress the potentials of disabled people. That is why the Handicraft Exhibition of Articles produced by disabled people and which the First Lady, Madam AHIDJO opened last Friday at the Red Cross headquarters in Yaounde is a step in the right direction. The seminar on the prevention and follow-up of disability which opens at the JOHN 23rd Centre in Mvolye, Yaounde immediately after the exhibition is another great idea.

These disabled people have abilities as well as disabilities and every one must be made aware that rehabilitation is based on the philosophy that what one can do is more important than what one cannot do. Wherever possible, disabled people would be helped to live at home as fully integrated members of their local communities. Yet, all of us want to do more than simply stay at home.

We want to get out to cultural, social and other events. Most of us also want to go out and work if we can. So too, disabled people, and access to the built environment is essential if they are to play their part in the normal activities of life. In fact, such access is as crucial to the enjoyment of a full and fulfilling life as all the aids and practical help which disabled people can be provided by a caring society.

And for the disabled, as for everyone else, "access" is not just about getting into and around public and social buildings. It has the much wider meaning of going somewhere and being accepted. We know how difficult it is to do everything at once for the disabled; all cannot be achieved at one go, which is why the international Year for Disabled People (IYDP) must be seen not just as a year that can soon be forgotten, but as the start of a new era.

Our concern must be to win for disabled people the opportunities that all other people take for granted. That is opportunities to work and to enjoy all kinds of human pursuits. In breaking down the social and architectural barriers, we shall also make it possible for disabled people to decide things for themselves instead of always having decisions made for them.

The International Year for Disabled People has been our best ever opportunity to get through the barriers of public indifference and ignorance to the lasting benefit of all disabled people. Everybody is therefore called upon to be of help to disabled persons. After all, bear in mind that every able-bodied person is a potential disabled person. Many persons were not born disabled. It happened at some point in time in their lives. Bear in mind that it could happen to any person at any time.

Mark Niboh

8

Cameroon Report 17/1/1982: Cameroon Nigeria Reconciliation

Introduction: *The news this week was undoubtedly President Ahmadou Ahidjo's four-day visit to Nigeria at the invitation of President Alhadji Shehu Shagari. For some time now, annual rotating visits have become customary for the leaders of Cameroon and Nigeria, serving as a framework for the appraisal of the state of bilateral relations and for prospecting further avenues of cooperation between the two neighbouring countries which share a lot in common, geographically and historically. George Ngwa reviews Cameroon-Nigeria relations against the background of a potentially explosive border incident.*

President AHIDJO's latest trip to Nigeria was a visit with a difference – coming as it was in the wake of a potentially explosive border incident in Cameroon's territorial waters in which five Nigerian soldiers lost their lives. That the two countries did not engage in a shooting war must be attributed to the foresightedness of their leaders and to the realisation that they stand more to lose than gain from giving jingoism a free reign.

All indications are that the unfortunate incident is a matter for history books; in fact, Presidents AHIDJO and SHAGARI made it clear in speeches at a banquet in honour of the visiting Cameroonian leader and in the communiqué marking the end of the visit. In their review of bilateral relations, the two leaders expressed regret at the border clash between the two countries last May and resolved not to allow the incident to affect cooperation between Nigeria and Cameroon.

The two Heads of State noted with satisfaction the frequent contacts existing between political and administrative authorities of the neighbouring regions of their two countries and urged the development of such friendly meetings.

President AHIDJO's visit, the communique went on, constituted an occasion for the two Heads of State to restore the atmosphere of confidence, peace and natural understanding between the two countries. Such statements as contained in the final communique can only be born of the belief that the greater dangers to peace lurk in insidious encroachments by men of zeal without any understanding and that, all and all, violence and war with their mingling of horror and heroism have the essential qualities of tragedy.

The decision by Presidents AHIDJO and SHAGARI to work towards burying the hatchet is testimony of the triumph of the olive branch over the sabre. Sabres we have, Sabres Nigerians have, but Cameroonians and Nigerians are not dogs whose first greeting to one another is a fight to determine who is stronger. Human beings are expected to work their hardest for peaceful coexistence because dogs do not need one another, but we do.

We see no more need for us to brandish our muscle than for a viper to advertise its fangs. Presidents AHIDJO and SHAGARI have shown that it takes maturity and magnanimity of spirit to react as they have in the face of all odds.

George Ngwa

9

Cameroon Report 02/2/1982: The Role of our Parliamentarians

Introduction: *For once, our members of Parliament have left their plush committee rooms and their equally plush residences to get a first-hand briefing on the problems faced by the people in the rural areas. News commentator Sam-Nuvala Fonkem sees the tour as another milestone in the country's political evolution.*

The fact that members of parliament have been given a chance to assess the political and socio-economic situation in different parts of the country other than their areas of origin, is a sign that we are in position to achieve in a long run, a political system which is devoid of sectarian and clannish tendencies and which is likely to attain a truly national character, a national character that supersedes the notion of political constituencies which are invariably plagued with nepotism, short-sightedness, and ethnocentric sentiments.

For the moment, we can view the exercise as experimental while hoping that the results of the exercise and the experience acquired will go a long way to bring about a convergence of ideas which of necessity should hinge around the notion of balanced development and social justice.

Observers are generally agreed on the fact that such an exercise can have no meaning if it is not centred on the concept of balanced development; thus our political representatives cannot claim to understand the concept of balanced development by divorcing themselves from the realities of the various regions of the country.

Being the representatives of the people and not some of the people, it is the parliamentarian's place to be constantly in touch with the development requirements of the various regions of the country so as to be able to properly deploy our national resources. This means that our members of parliament have to go beyond a mere bureaucratic assessment of our development requirements to be in a position to decide on the distribution of our national resources. They have to make an on-the-spot assessment, learn from the political grassroots the actual needs of the people as well as their strong and weak points.

Just to cite an example, there were sufficient indications that the group of parliamentarians that visited the Eastern Province took special note of the lack of community development initiatives, a notion which is quite new east of the Mungo, the lack of which compromises our self-reliant development policy.

It is our fervent hope that the knowledge and experience gathered by the parliamentarians during their familiarisation tour would be well documented and made public for future references and guidelines and that the exercise should be more frequent and should encompass the most remote areas of our national territory.

Such knowledge should not, of course end at documentation and publication but should be effectively used as a base for enlightenment on future policy making procedures – that is to say the public expects decisions on policy to be better informed and unbiased.

In other words, the absence of a well-informed decision making process may likely give the impression that familiarisation tours by members of parliament are a mere occasion for entertainment and sight-seeing. Entertainment and sight-seeing are certainly very healthy exercises, physically, morally and socially, but we still have to be convinced that they are not the main objectives of the exercise. This leads to the question of the role of the Member of Parliament and how much of his time and energy must be sacrificed for the accomplishment of the task that is expected of him.

Some observers feel that it is time that the job of a parliamentarian becomes a full-time occupation and should not only limit itself to the occasional attendance of ordinary and extra-ordinary sessions of parliament. Like the executive and judiciary, the legislature should operate with equal regularity and consistency so as to enable parliamentarians have a sense of continual duty to the population.

Members of parliament like all civil servants have constant remuneration throughout their term of office and it is only right that they should earn and deserve this remuneration by a constant application to the task that is required of them namely, to be able to devote sufficient time to the study of bills tabled before parliament and assess the accountability of public officers, and agencies, corporations and companies.

The notion that members of parliament are bench-warmers and hand clappers is still very strong in the minds of the public and it is only by going a step further in their activities that we can start believing in the mastery of our destiny.

Sam- Nuvala Fonkem

10

Cameroon Report 06/6/1982: Wastage and Mismanagement in Public Health Services

Introduction: *For several years, the budget of the Ministry of Public Health has remained the third largest of all government departments. Despite these vast financial outlays made each year, our health services do not seem to improve and in some cases have even deteriorated. This week, senior staff of the Ministry came together for a seminar on how to cut down waste and improve hospital management. Julius Wamey examines the theme of the seminar and tries to see what went wrong with our health services:*

There is a time honoured adage which holds that "health is wealth". I have no intention of quarrelling with such wisdom as is contained in this ancient saying except to point out that it is increasingly losing its relevance to life in the space age.

These days, with the cost of keeping oneself fit and healthy becoming ever more prohibitive, you and Mr. John Citizen next door are finding out that the reverse of this adage holds true. These days "wealth is health".

This is a crushing revelation to those of us who have committed the unpardonable crime of being in that part of the globe hat has been classified, in space age medical language, as the 'disease infested Third World'.

We not only have to import pollution and exotic diseases from the industrialised "First World", but we must also import the drugs with which to fight those diseases from the same source. And since we have no pharmaceutical industry to speak of, we have as little say over the prices we pay for these imported drugs we need so desperately as we have over the raw materials we export for their manufacture.

This has placed Third World governments in a dilemma out of which they can see no immediate release and Cameroon is one of them.

Fully aware of this problem, our government finds the current waste of drugs, money and general mismanagement in our health institutions doubly painful. Mr Citizen finds such waste a sacrilege and a scandal.

You have no doubt heard stories of how tons of medicines are thrown away in our hospitals while patients die away slowly because there are no drugs for them. The stories are, on the most part, perfectly true but these medicines are not always thrown away because the government wants you to pay for them or out of sheer wickedness as some people claim. We lose these milliards of francs worth of drugs due entirely to short-sighted planning and mismanagement.

When calling for a mastery of modern management techniques and the elimination of waste in the administration of our hospitals, Minister of Health, Eteme Oloa must have had this outrageous state of affairs in mind.

I talk of mismanagement when our health authorities order expensive and extremely perishable drugs with no precise notion of how to store them and without the adequate storage facilities. A few days after they arrive from Europe, they are being thrown away as having "expired".

There is mismanagement when our authorities are either deceived or bribed to order drugs which already exist in the country under a different brand name. Most often these drugs are either exported to us to be experimented with for the first time on black patients or have been banned in their countries of manufacture as unfit for use by humans.

Doctors also contribute to the miseries of Mr Citizen when they prescribe five different drugs for him where one would do the job. It is alleged that many of our doctors receive a percentage of the price paid to pharmacists for the drugs thus prescribed.

Behind this alarming sickness of our health institutions are the big multinational drug companies which are more concerned with profits than with the health of Mr. John Citizen.

These companies are ready to lie, cheat, deceive and bribe government officials in order to sell their products and turn a profit.

Drugs, however, are only part of the problem. What is to be said about hospitals where money is allocated for feeding destitute patients and yet one never sees a plate of hospital-cooked food in the wards? Where the staff carry home the food, the bedding, the soap, the toilet paper, and even the drugs meant for patients; where store-keepers and other health administrators grow fat on the misery of the sick.

Maladministration in our hospitals concerns not only the waste in drugs but also misuse of medical staff and equipment – all of which make a messy situation even messier.

A few seminars for health technicians and other personnel may not be enough but it is a start toward reversing this trend in our medical institutions. The change, however, should be fundamental and start from the top with a profound study of our drug and equipment importation policy as a priority. We may have no say over the prices we pay for our drugs but we should be able to decide the quality and quantity of what we are buying. This at least would help to eliminate waste.

As for what can be done to make hospital management more efficient, we can only appeal to health administrators, as we have appealed to administrators of other services in past programmes, to work not with an eye on personal gain but with their consciences on human suffering. Railing against corruption and lack of duty consciousness is nothing new on this programme and we would like to avoid sounding repetitive.

As has been said, staying healthy these days is an expensive business and we are well aware of the government's effort to ease the burden for Mr. And Mrs. Citizen. Every Cameroonian has the right to feel scandalised when he sees our scarce resources going down the drain.

Julius Wamey

11

Cameroon Report 01/10/1982: Crackdown on Customs Fraud

Introduction: *Turning now to other event of the week, there was the customs fraud affair. Every citizen in this country will agree with us (Cameroon Report) that the man who once drank soda or tonic water switches immediately to Becks beer or St. Pauli Girl on becoming a Customs Officer. This exhibition of their ill-gotten riches obviously leads to social emulation by less scrupulous members of the society, constituting a serious and constant threat to public morality. This observation leads one to recall with nostalgia, the good old days of West Cameroon when commissions of inquiry were set up to probe people who become rich overnight. People tend to regard these customs officials with contempt including those in the lower grades, some of whom are said to own mansions, hotels and other businesses. Ask a customs officer where he acquired his wealth, he would not give you an answer, but the forces of law and order found out recently. The discovery is believed to have marked a new era for Becks drinkers – facing justice behind the bars. Businessmen were arrested and jailed, irrespective of where they come from. Now citizens are beginning to feel that the lawlessness in this country, usually carried out with the complicity of those who are supposed to uphold the law has entered a critical phase. NGOBESING SUH ROMNUS is somehow very optimistic about the recent crackdown on customs fraud in the port city of Douala and says the fight against crime in the society must take horizontal and vertical dimensions for it to become effective:*

Action has for once, without wasting any time, crowned our words. In this New Year address to the Cameroon nation on December 31, 1981, our Head of State, President AMADOU AHIDJO lashed out against the canker worms that have been eating into our society. The President vehemently condemned social vices such as bribery and corruption, fraud, misappropriation of public funds, tax evasion and lack of professional consciousness. At the same time he assured the Cameroon people he and the government would crush the monsters when and wherever they are found.

Perhaps only a few people, as usual, were convinced that this time business was meant. Yes, President AHIDJO meant business and one could detect it from his tone. It was not the traditional political poetry to which many people are too used to. It was not the poetry that has lulled people to sleep in the past while the holocaust continued unchecked.

Immediately after his message to the nation, the Head of State and government moved ahead to put the words into action. There was a crack down on a number of business crooks and irresponsible, unreliable and fraudulent customs officers who took the Cameroon law into their hands importing goods worth hundreds of millions of francs and manoeuvring to escape customs duty. What a big loss that was going to be to government! And what a big shame to the frauds! These twenty-two thieves were tracked down and severely punished by law.

The Minister of Justice and authorities of the judicial and legal department in Douala as well as the forces of law and order need to be lauded for tracing and capturing the swindlers. Because justice prevailed this time and the law exercised with neither fear nor favour, the frauds were condemned to many years of imprisonment and heavy fines.

We know that criminals have been embezzling or defrauding money or goods in this way in the country and living the lifestyles of millionaires. These are the same thieves who have mansions here and there. They have hundreds of millions in their bank accounts, buy cars and build homes for girl friends and worse of all, crush the poor and helpless ones whose money they actually stole to become what they are.

When you think of all these and the many more atrocities they cause because of their ill-begotten wealth, you will not help praising the authorities for the measures taken against these frauds. This is a step in the right direction, but it is only a step and we cannot now sit back and feel that all that needs to be done has been done. It is only a beginning that should serve as a warning to all those worms that eat us from within, all those money mongers and tax evaders that their crime life span has been shortened dramatically.

No tax inspector should under tax a business tycoon again with a view to receiving a big bribe and hope to go free. No stores accountant should try to defraud government's money by asking a seller to issue false bills and hope to go free.

People who have been entrusted with government budgets and have embezzled the money, people who sell examination questions, steal and sell certificates, those who receive bribe in order to put Mr. X into category nine instead of category four, those who think that they can make telephone calls and solve all their problems illegally, in short, all those who disobey the law and go against the ethics of society should be prepared to face their doom when it comes. The crackdown has just begun and we expect it to continue with more stringency.

We are aware of the fact that criminals like the ones we have been talking about usually think they can break the law and go free either because they are cunning or because they think that when matters come to a head, they would use some of the fraudulent money to buy themselves out of penalty. Well, they have failed to do so now as the Douala case testifies. So, those of you who may be nursing plans of embezzlement and fraud should not think you are any smarter than the Douala gang. You will also fail and will be unsympathetically dealt with.

We know, and the forces of law and order know, and most people in society know that frauds, tax evaders, in fact all criminals in society always seek new means of carrying out their malicious deeds when the old tricks are uncovered. Yet they must know that the new ones will still be discovered. The saying rightly goes that nothing can be hidden under the sun and that leaves have ears. All those people could be tracked down in a week if a search were carried out.

We do hope that the forces of law and order, in collaboration with authorities in the judicial and legal departments will continue as they have done in the case of the twenty-two frauds in Douala, to transform the President's words into action by tracking down all these bad seeds and punishing them severely.

The fight against fraud and corruption must assume horizontal and vertical dimensions so that these criminals may be completely uprooted from the society.

Ngobesing Romanus

12

Cameroon Report 24/10/1982, FONADER: Not yet the Farmer's Bank

Introduction: *Installing the newly-appointed Director-General of the National Fund for Rural Development, FONADER, the Minister of Agriculture spoke of the need to transform the fund into a real farmer's bank. SAM-NUVALA FONKEM is of the opinion that there wouldn't be any grounds for such an appeal if there wasn't the strong feeling that FONADER was not fulfilling its mission, namely to boost agricultural production and upgrade the standard of living in rural areas by making loans available to farmers on a rational basis:*

Installing the newly-appointed Director General of FONADER, the Minister of Agriculture conceded that the previous management which pioneered the fund was plagued by the usual problems affecting most enterprises at the early stages.

These problems include inadequate financial resources to meet growing demands, ill-adapted and unrealistic conditions for granting agricultural loans for specific projects, and a sloppy management of finances and personnel.

In what was clearly a prescription for FONADER's ailments, the Minister outlined measures taken or about to be taken to enable the fund fulfil its mission. These include a general clean-up of intervention units charged with the deployment of credits in rural areas, an internal reorganisation of FONADER, better training programmes for staff and a healthy management for cooperatives. Other measures

41

include stepping up the campaign for the repayment of loans and the setting up of a viable accounting system.

The Minister also appealed to the population not to regard FONADER merely as an institution for dispensing credits to farmers but also as an intermediary for government subsidies to the agricultural sector and foreign investments. As a government intermediary, it handles phytosanitary campaigns, distributes subsidies for fertilizers and is involved in the setting up of Young Farmers' Groups and village water projects.

Given present forecast, the Minister went on, Cameroon's population should be around 14 million by the year 2000 with un urban population of between 3 and 7 million. Needless to say such an urban population growth would be explosive with a ratio of one peasant providing food for about eight urban dwellers. To check this situation, agricultural production would have to grow at a rate of 40% per year as opposed to the present 5 %.

Agricultural credits may increase within the year but this objective may prove to be an uphill task if the recovery of agricultural loans continues to be slow and delinquent.

Granted that greater financial resources could be made in future to meet public demands, the entire mission of FONADER may end up in failure if there are no fixed modalities for a rational distribution of credits on a regional quota basis.

An irrational distribution of agricultural credits which up till now are usually obtained by absentee landlords who are far removed from the plight of rural communities and by wheeler-dealers whose only collateral is a visiting card obtained from a political big shot or a real estate charlatan and who usually has no other intention beyond gratifying his taste for all the latest automobiles and splendid mansions. Such a distribution system can only end up bolstering the weight of an empty, materialistic, bourgeoisie whose growth continues to be a liability to the nation.

Sam-Nuvala Fonkem

13

Cameroon Report 24/10/1982: Mount Cameroon Erupts

Introduction: *On Friday October 15, 1982, Chief Gervasius Mbella Endeley, paramount chief of the Bakweri tribe, located at the foot of Mount Cameroon, died in his Buea palace at the age of 85. His burial book place on Sunday October 17 and as CAMTIMES news magazine reported: "Barely a few hours into nightfall, the Cameroon Mountain erupted and vibrated, casting flames into the skyline. Thereafter, there were blasts like a volley of gunfire." Mount Cameroon, with the highest peak in West Africa (4070 metres) has erupted five times in this century: 1909, 1922, 1954, 1959 and 1982. Reports said the volcano erupted from two craters at a height of 3,400 meters. Experts on the scene said the craters were spitting out lava, pebbles, and ashes into the atmosphere. They said the lava flowed towards the west coast villages of Bakingili and Isokolo in a 300 metre-wide track, burning trees and vegetation. Although no lives were lost, contingency measures were taken to evacuate villages along the path of the lava. Legend among the Bakweris holds that the eruption is related to the death of the chief and the tribe is said to have performed certain traditional rites to appease the anger of the mountain god, Epasa Moto. Scientists, however, hold a different view as there is sufficient data to illustrate that the mountain is an active volcano whose volcanicity dates back to 100 million years. Mr. Vincent Azobi, Lecturer of Physical Geography at the Bilingual High School in Yaounde prepared this report on the volcanic nature and history of mount Cameroon:*

Mount Cameroon, Fako Mountain or Buea Mountain as the natives prefer to call it, is a composite volcanic structure built through successive eruptions. Early occurrences, through a single central vent are known to have been very violent, throwing ash and other products distances away. Huge lava layers pile up and seal the main outlet at the top of the mountain so that subsequent eruptions could occur only through fissures of subsidiary vents at the flanks (of the mountain) as is the case with the present eruption. The formation of Mount Cameroon is linked to the building of an extensive chain of volcanic mountains from the coast, through the Western High Plateau to the Adamaoua. This chain of mountains lies along a great fault line extending from the Island of Sao Tome and Principe in the Atlantic, to Fernando Po, then into Cameroon and across to the Tibesti mountains in Northern Chad.

Volcanism here is therefore not unconnected to this fracture which created weak zones in the crust. The event can be dated at about 100 million years ago when generalised rocking movements shook the earth and tore parts of it away (continental drift).

Mount Cameroon actually began to take shape less than two million years ago. Volcanic eruptions on mount Cameroon are not a recent phenomenon. About the year 600 B.C., HANNO, the famous Carthaginian navigator had discovered this mountain in eruption, describing it as the "Chariot of the Gods". Portuguese explorers of the West Coast of Africa had the same experience in the 15th century when they saw on the continent, "Great fire lifting unto the skies".

During our century, Mount Cameroon is known to have erupted several times, once in 1909, then in 1922, 1954, 1959 and recently (1982). Traces of the 1959 eruption can be seen behind Ekona Mbenge where thicknesses of lava have solidified, fondly referred to by people of that area as "fire burn".

Apart from actual eruptions, the restive interior of Fako Mountain has often expressed itself in the form of tremors such as occurred some three years ago, causing much panic in the region. Earth tremors can precede, accompany or occur independently of eruption. When they are not accompanied by eruptions, then the volcano must have been consumed within the earth. Sometimes, earth tremors announce an imminent earthquake.

Mount Cameroon is an active volcanic mountain. Judging from the recent frequency of volcanic eruptions here, we can yet expect many more of them. What is important in the case of Mount Fako, however, is that fissure eruptions are not usually violent. Also, the very gently nature of lava flow emitted from it can make us conclude that all else may be erased, the Fako type of volcano cannot overwhelm people, except, perhaps that we are dealing with uncontrollable forces.

Vincent Azobi

14

Cameroon Report 7/11/1982: President Ahmadou Ahidjo's Dramatic Resignation

Introduction: *On November 4th 1982, Cameroonians who tuned to Radio Cameroon's 8 pm news heard the news of their life, a news item that came as a shock to many who had come to accept president AHIDJO as an unproclaimed life President. Mr. AHIDJO announced his sudden and unexpected resignation after nearly a quarter century at the head of the nation, quitting office at the age of 58. President AHIDJO handed over power to his constitutional successor Prime Minister PAUL BIYA. These are Mr AHIDJO's words of resignations:*

Cameroonians,
Fellow Countrymen,

I have decided to resign from my duties as President of the United Republic of Cameroon. This decision takes effect on Saturday, November 6, 1982 at 10 am.

In this crucial moment, I wish, and from the bottom of my heart, to express my gratitude to all who have, for almost twenty-five years now, accorded me their confidence and assistance in the accomplishment of the heavy duties at the helm of this nation.

On the other hand, I wish to express my thanks particularly to militants of our great national party – the Cameroon National Union, for their unswerving, constant and total support.

If much is left to be done in the noble task of building our beloved and dear country which we have accomplished together since independence and re-unification, considerable progress has been achieved in all areas.

Our country now has great potentials: national unity consolidated, numerous varied and complementary resources, an ever expanding economy, healthy finances, appreciable social justice, a hard working population and a dynamic youth, solid and fruitful relations of friendship and cooperation in Africa and the world.

I invite all Cameroonians to accord without reserve, their confidence and collaboration to my constitutional successor, Mr. PAUL BIYA. He deserves the confidence of everyone at home and abroad.

I implore you to remain united, patriotic, hard-working and a worthy, dynamic and respectable people.

I pray, the Lord Almighty to continue to grant Cameroonians the necessary help and protection in their development efforts, in peace, unity and justice.

Long Live Cameroon

CR Coordinator: *No man in the world has more courage than the man who can stop after eating one peanut. AHMADOU AHIDJO had that courage to stop after eating twenty-four. He gave no clues as to why he was resigning. It was vintage AHIDJO politics: discrete and mysterious to the end. A swift decision to resign and hand over power in 48 hours would, in most countries, rock the ship of state and perhaps lead to irredeemable chaos. But in Cameroon, it has so far been smooth and will remain as such, we hope, for a very long time to come, thanks to the mechanism of succession embodied in article 7 section 4 of the nation's constitution. LUKE ANANGA has these observations:*

In this country, and in recent times, dramatic events crop up that continue to befuddle detractors, particularly foreign political analysts. The sudden announcement last Thursday of the resignation of President AHIDJO is obviously the most serious case in the history of this country. Within 48 hours, President AHIDJO was ready to leave and in the shortest statement on record to the nation, he bid good-bye, announced his successor as provided for by the constitution, and exhorted every Cameroonian to unite behind Mr. PAUL BIYA because, as he put it, he deserves it and because as Cameroonians, it is in our habit and tradition to stand firm behind our leaders.

The same detractors listening to this opinion are likely to brand it a premature assessment of the swiftness and continuity in terms of succession in this country. To think so, however, is to portray abysmal ignorance of the degree of maturity of the Cameroonian people and the point they have reached in terms of their mastery of contemporary history.

Perhaps one or two cases will indicate our stand point. In spite of the long history and the unremitting bombast about their political stability and continuity, which presupposes a smooth transition in leadership in the United States, it takes three months – from November to January for this transition to take place. In Senegal, where the precedent was set on the African continent by SEDAR SENGHOR, with the dramatic announcement of his resignation, it took at least one month for his successor, ABDOU DIOUF to be named for him to take office.

Once again and back here in 48 hours, President AHIDJO was set to leave and in keeping with constitutional guarantees, his successor, PAUL BIYA was known and did assume office yesterday. It is a credible hall mark of the accomplishment of the arduous task President AHIDJO and the people of this country set out to achieve twenty-five years ago, namely: to create such stable political, judicial, administrative, and economic institutions as would make transition from one government to the other, from one personality to the other, not only smooth but also iconoclastically swift. And in the process of the creation of these national institutions, care was taken to completely destroy the notion of indispensability – in other words, the notion that after AHIDJO there would be a deluge.

While we agree that this is a predictable trend in the history of leadership crisis in the third world, credit and enormous credit for that matter, ought to be given to the outgoing head of state, AHMADOU AHIDJO, for his brilliant guidance which has made us by-pass this regrettable limbo through which many African countries have passed.

Cameroonians take comfort in three-dimensional factor: firstly that Mr. AHIDJO's wisdom and fore-sight will remain available to his successor PAUL BIYA as AHIDJO is still the national President of the Cameroon National Union Party; secondly that his successor, PAUL BIYA is an unbending graduate of the school of thought that has guided this country for twenty-five years; thirdly and finally that the people of this country hold their development so dearly and treasure the fatherland so immeasurably that they could not be expected to do anything to jeopardise this continuity and stability – all three factors contained in President AHIDJO's decision to resign.

Luke Ananga

15

Cameroon Report 7/11/1982: The Task Ahead for President Paul Biya

Introduction: *In his inaugural speech yesterday, Mr. AHIDJO's successor, His Excellency PAUL BIYA vowed to respect and safeguard the constitution, ensure continuity in all the political options of the Cameroon National Union Party and the government. In short, he pledged to stay on the course charted by former President AHIDJO. President BIYA showed his dedication to this pledge last night when he appointed thirty-five-year-old BELLO BOUBA MAIGARI of the North as Prime Minister and reshuffled the cabinet without throwing anyone out. Nevertheless, President BIYA has much to do. For one thing, he replaces somebody who quit power at the summit of his career and that's the problem many Cameroonians and foreigners are anxiously watching to see i.e. how PAUL BIYA will meet the challenge.*
ERIC CHINJE has this analysis:

The last moment was breath-taking! In a terse, solemn speech, memorable, historic, unprecedented for Cameroon, unique for Africa, AHMADOU AHIDJO called it quits. A gaping, doubting, questioning Cameroon had to accept the inevitable: one generation had come, lived its time, brought its contribution to the timeless grind of history and, in the quiet words of AMADOU AHIDJO, made its exit from the centre-stage. The spotlight moves, and the show must go on.

On the scene, Mr. PAUL BIYA, surrounded by a redoubtable group of well-schooled and disciplined team players, the talk is of continuity, of peace, of unity, of all

53

those cardinal elements of progress upon which the nation's first President so successfully predicated his rule. There are prayers for the new leaders, expressions of best wishes, and hopes for a future as glorious, as resplendent, and full of achievement as in the Republic's past two decades.

The excitement is over, and euphoria must make way for some cool and level-headed thinking. Some hard questions, some difficult answers! Independence, reunification and unification; peace, stability and progress – the case for the past is closed. The new chapter must begin and we must ask loud and clear: where do we go from here? The question is unavoidable. The outside world is eager for some straight answers. Investors, who only a few days ago had Cameroon on the best-market list, are eager for some straight answers. Political pundits, who made of Cameroon the very quintessence of stability and peace in Africa, are eager, eager to read the movement of the indicator on this nation's political barometer. Out there, everyone is hopeful, everyone is expectant, anticipative.

Back in Cameroon, the theatre of all action, speculation must give room to the hard, cold, realities that confront the nation. Peace and stability in the last quarter century were founded on the solid bedrock of a fairly equitable distribution nationwide of the treasures of the land: of economic prosperity, of political power, of social advantages, of economic opportunity. Will this continue to be the case?

Will Akwaya and Mulundu, Mora and Ndikinimiki, Bukwango and Essimbi become even more fully integrated in the national development effort? All indications are to the positive but those indications do not mute some popular concerns, especially among the majority of this programme, Cameroon Report's national audience. There are obvious questions about the places that English and French continue to occupy in the national linguistic package.

Is one heading for linguistic oblivion, destined to be effaced and replaced by the other? Or will bilingualism rebound and the rampant social use of the unflattering "Anglo" or "Frog" be forced out of our proletarian vocabulary?

On the question of regional development, will the gathering mould of stagnation, decay and neglect that hangs over once vibrant urban communities as Limbe, Kumba, Mamfe and Bamenda dissipate? Will the man in Fako feel even more a part of the SONARA reality than he has been wont to feel?

On the issue of regional leadership, will the new leader exhibit that same rare aptitude for selecting regional leaders and will these leaders serve President BIYA by being more vocal about the needs and the yearnings of their people than they have been wont to be? Will the problems of Meme, Manyu, Donga-Mantung and Menchum be aired, vociferously, by those accorded the distinguished duty of airing them?

Former President AHIDJO said in his last words that the path is long and the task is immense. A lot has been accomplished; a lot can be accomplished. We are living now a period of wait, hope, and see. It can be a better future, but the present must be taken on boldly, without reserve, with frankness, with a positive attitude to redress any existing wrongs. Hope is the watchword.

Eric Chinje

16

Cameroon Report 28/11/1982: Biya and the Housing Crisis

Introduction: *Barely a fortnight after his accession to office, President Paul Biya has issued instructions to the authorities concerned to take concrete action to solve the housing crisis. Opening the 5th Council of the Cameroon National Union party, President Biya frowned at the inadequacy of housing units which he said, were not adapted to the African family structure. Shortly after the President's declarations, the Housing Minister took up the chorus and disclosed plans for setting up more housing units. While plans to satisfy the ever increasing housing needs are being implemented, Victor Epie Ngome says the most urgent measure that must be taken is the regulation of house rents:*

It always seems to take forever for the plight of the robins and the starlings in the grass to hit the eye of the eagle perched up in the baobab but when that does happen, it is always greeted with a fresh wave of hope.

And when shortly after that, the housing boss broke the official tradition of silence and pours what is tantamount to a torrent into the press about what government is doing to offset the crisis, even more hope waves were set in motion.

One thing about hope is that if misguided, it could lead to dangerous speculation, followed by deflation-desperation after the torrent; many Cameroonians are likely to carry their nets out into the streets, forgetting that rainwater does not contain fish, although it could eventually be collected into a pond and seeded with fish fry.

Nevertheless, it was good to hear that we would soon get a gig and progressive increase in housing facilities in our main urban centres and we can start thinking, even if wishfully, that these houses will be given to those who deserve them most, judging by the nature of their work, and not by their sex, origin or contacts.

It was good to hear that SIC will no longer have a monopoly of housing contracts in the country and everyone knows that a certain amount of competition, with good conscientious refereeing, is bound to bring housing cost down and lever up the quality of facilities because SIC's low-cost housing is everything but low cost for its standards. We could only add that these new competitors need not be foreign – when there are nationals like Nangah, Fonjungo, and a host of others ready for services. It was good to hear that government will now make it easier for Cameroonians to build their own houses, the land being prepared before hand and then sold to them, and that they will be able to pay, thanks to the Housing Loans Fund Scheme. It would have been better still to hear of new steps towards ensuring that you will no longer have to be super citizen to be able to grind out these loans.

But as it has been rightly observed, it will take time for these measures to offset the housing crisis even one tenth of the way.

While waiting for this to happen, the bulk of the population will have to continue to depend on private landlords to meet their immediate needs. It is even impossible to expect that at one time in the foreseeable future, everyone will either be lodged in a government house or in houses of their own, not even on the assumption that there will be no more transfers so that when you build your house, in say

Douala, you work there until you retire. Suppose you are not a civil servant? Suppose you are self-employed?

Whatever you do, the private landlord still has a role to play and as at now, this role is that of a greedy speculator and almighty extortioner. A house, no matter how hastily and sloppily constructed, no matter how badly it is maintained, is a gold-mine which must solve all the owner's financial problems. For the tenant, it is usually a take-or-leave deal, which is no choice since he is always too stranded to leave it.

This is what I called the plight of the robbin and the starling and it was good to hear the Head of State vent his concern over it. And it was good to hear the Minister begin to admit, even if only as a second thought, that there was need to control rents. What wasn't half as good to hear was the palpable emphasis on the inconveniences of regulating these rents and special mention was made of the difficulty of policing landlords and the risk of fiscal fraud. Well, it looks like there just was a need to say something.

If we know that every house in town has a number – given at the census, and that for every new one, there is a building permit, and if we know how close we have succeeded in bringing the administration to the people, then how can our rent policy really be so hard to police? Fiscal fraud is a big evil for sure, but we have not stopped levying customs duties because we fear fraud or tax evasion because there would always be evaders. We don't lack ways of making people abide by laws made in the national interest.

This reporter thinks that the alternative to rent control is anarchy and from the social, economic and political standpoint, the consequences of any slops we make in our choice, are too ghastly to contemplate. Rents have to be controlled. There are no two ways to do it. This could be on the basis of the quality of the house and its location, both of which are known to the urban or housing authorities. Whether it be at parastatal level, the housing situation definitely can do with some retouching, to say the least and this need for retouching seems to have set the government thinking of late. And concerning the measures that have been proposed, many of them very laudable, this reporter thinks that there could be a shift in emphasis. He thinks that while it is necessary to build more houses and to encourage competition among building companies, it is by far more necessary to regulate the present rental rate.

Victor Epie Ngome

17

Cameroon Report 9/7/1983: Our Ailing Parastatal Corporations

Introduction: *The President of the National Assembly Honourable S.T. MUNA closed the annual budgetary session with a strong warning to public corporations that government subsidies to them would henceforth become the exception rather than the rule. News commentator SAM-NUVALA FONKEM sees the warning as the highest public denunciation of unprofitable corporations and examines the mismanagement and financial malpractice plaguing these establishments:*

The recent call by the President of the National Assembly for more productivity in statutory corporations implies that these bodies have not been productive enough and when he goes further to stress the need for these corporations to become more viable and profitable, warning that future government subsidies to them would be the exception rather than the rule, one is bound to understand that many of these corporations have generally depended on government to keep their heads above water and that apart from being unprofitable, they have become more of a liability than an asset to the state.

The attention drawn to the problems of statutory corporations by the Speaker of the House is so far the most emphatic reference by any top ranking authority to this long-standing problem which calls for an urgent examination and probe into the activities of these establishments. The situation also warrants a revision of the management and managerial methods of corporations, an approach which falls within a range of possible measures that might include the dissolution of some corporations with an irredeemably bad record.

Good management of parastatal organisations requires a judicious and rational deployment of financial and human resources aimed at productivity and profitability of the public good, not the private good of the individuals who administer such bodies.

It is public knowledge that the bulk of the funds allocated to run statutory corporations is visibly squandered in providing for the petty indulgences of executive staff. By petty indulgences, this reporter is not referring to fringe benefits and justifiable miscellaneous expenditures, but is talking here of the lavish cocktail parties, frequent pleasure trips abroad under the pretext of official business, graft practices in the ordering of supplies (a widely accepted practice involving the inflation of invoices), direct misappropriation of funds and the diversion of corporate property and equipment for private businesses.

All of the above do not constitute a legal charge against any given corporation, but both the layman and the multitude of adventurous contractors would tell you how such and such a big shot got his latest Mercedes car from such a such a contract, maintains children in universities abroad and has just completed a 40 million francs luxury villa, probably his fourth since becoming financial director or manager of such and such a parastatal.

Gross mismanagement is not confined to just the petty indulgences of executive staff, but like in agro-industrial bodies, it has consisted in a thin pay-packet and a pinched expression for the labourers, all of which do not enhance the spirit of productivity.

Poor management can also be seen in the wide disparity in salaries between national and expatriates, the latter enjoying unjustifiable facilities such as compensation for the cost and convenience of buying European food in Africa – a ridiculous notion indeed which does not even equal the ludicrous idea of providing allowances for pet food and veterinary care for the pets of expatriate cadres. If one cannot see the need to check the swell in expatriate salaries at least we must see the need, if only in keeping with our policy of social justice, to close the wide gap in salaries in all the various economic sectors of the country.

Urgent measures to salvage corporations would be to redefine objectives – an exercise which some observers think would entail the eradication of some public and parastatal organisations which are not only unproductive, but which have outlived their usefulness or are a cunning duplication of other parastatals.

The significant role parastatals play in development and their immense control of the vital structures of economic development, calls for austere measures that would have to move away from the previous paternalistic notion of management to a management based on rational economic principles and social responsibility.

Sam-Nuvala Fonkem

Cameroon Report 6/8/1983: The University as Brain Trust

Introduction: *A three day national symposium on the evaluation of primary health care projects was held this week at the Yaounde University Centre for Health Sciences (CUSS). Opening the symposium, the Director of CUSS Professor Eben Moussi said the constant evaluation of government projects enhances accuracy in the planning and execution of future projects. In this light, the Director also spoke of the vital role of the University in the generation of new ideas. In the commentary coming up, SAM-NUVALA FONKEM examines the implication of the above statements with regard to the role of the University as a source of information and knowledge indispensable for the* daily *running of national affairs:*

The impression most people have about the University today is still regrettably influenced by a monastic concept of education, hence the view of the University as a cold-storage for rusticated minds engaged in academic tedium with an intellectual eccentricity and a scholastic indifference which merely stops short of misanthropy.

That indeed is some old time religion which was good for the ancient scribes and monks, but not good enough for the fast changing world of today. Today we speak of dynamism as opposed to inertia, active participation as opposed to indifference.

Very recently there has been an on-going debate in the national daily newspaper, Cameroon Tribune, on the Cameroonian intellectual and freedom of expression. This reporter would not go into the interesting ramifications of this debate, but would simply remark that the fact that the topic of freedom of expression is causing an unprecedented open debate and an abundant flow of ink, indicates that for a very long while, the Cameroonian intellectual has been deliberately or inadvertently constrained to embrace silence and indifference as a result of a certain degree of ideological intolerance which characterised the era before now. This is merely an observation, not a conclusion, since a circumstantial intellectual debate does not necessarily mean a radical change of mentality.

We can only start hoping for a change of mentality when an institution like the University is restored its academic freedom and financial autonomy as opposed to managerial autonomy. This freedom must of course be accompanied by obligations which could be summed up as a dynamic participation in national development and the day to day running of national affairs.

This, I suppose, is what the Director of CUSS meant when he spoke of the vital role of the University in the generation of new ideas which in this reporter's opinion must be reckoned with by the authorities.

The University should serve as a think-tank for the policy making process and should be effectively used to study crucial problems in the areas of culture, art, science and technology. A significant number of intellectuals, promising scholars, geniuses and visionaries alike have been compelled to either drown their academic lethargy or given voice to their intellectual frustrations in beer parlours which (unlike the coffee houses of 19th century Britain), have served as grounds for escapism.

Ideas can grow under some of the most unexpected circumstances and unlikely places, including beer parlours, but if such unlikely places could serve as one of the most convenient forums for social interaction and exchange of ideas, such likelihood could be jeopardised if social forums become exhibition centres for academic distinctions and intellectual medals.

Academic distinctions are as good as honorary medals as long as the bearers indulge in intellectual complacency as well as social and academic banalities which do nothing to promote knowledge or development. Intellectual conceit can be tolerated as long as it does not degenerate into personal advertisement, self-aggrandisement and social banalities such as inter-personal or inter-tribal antagonisms.

When the intellectuals themselves must have taken a profound self-criticism and a change of attitude towards the concept of intellectualism, then we may start hoping for a more dynamic role of academic institutions, particularly the University, in the modernisation process.

Sam-Nuvala Fonkem

19

Cameroon Report 31/3/1984: Biya on Housing and Road Construction

Introduction: *Last Friday's cabinet meeting which focused on the housing and road construction issues in the country came up with certain pertinent observations indicating that the Head of State is not only quite conversant with the issues, but refuses to be blindfolded by the usual All-correct, No-problem progress reports presented by government officials. SAM-NUVALA FONKEM has more on the issue:*

Commenting on reports presented on the low-cost housing programme, the Head of State frowned at delays in the execution of housing projects, a glaring practice already observed by the man-in-the-street.

The President gave strict instructions to the Housing Ministry to study ways of diversifying and liberalising the real estate sector, a solution which Cameroon Report has gone a long way in the past years to stress as the most sensible way of breaking the ancient monopoly of the Housing Corporation whose housing units are anything but low-cost, and whose lethargy and inability to meet increasing demands are well-known.

In recommending the diversification and opening of the real estate sector to both indigenous and foreign entrepreneurs, we would want to suggest that preference be given to nationals.

The Head of State also recommended the reduction of the cost of housing construction and one would imagine, of course, that something must be done about the cost of land and building materials. We would like to suggest a reduction, if not a freeze on the prices of these items.

President BIYA also had some very good news for local construction firms, such as the dismantling of administrative bottlenecks in the payment of bills to entrepreneurs and softening conditions and guarantees involved in the award of public contracts. Although it was not always said, delays in construction projects are not only due to incompetent and delinquent construction firms, but also complications and delays in the payment of bills by the administrations.

It is not very clear how the President intends to bring down road construction costs, but the decision to give the Military Engineering Corps, a greater role in the programme can be said to be in the right direction and would give the corps a more dynamic participation in national development.

A complementary measure would be to pay more attention to the malpractice of over-invoicing by firms and entrepreneurs who would be satisfied with nothing less than a 300 % profit margin. This also leads to the question of kick-backs and this is where we expect the anti-corruption programme to become effectively operational.

In all, the cabinet debates on the construction issue clearly echoed public disenchantment with weaknesses in that sector and also came up with bold and unprecedented recommendations which one supposes would be followed to the letter by the administration.

Since the Head of State cannot be everywhere at every time to supervise every banal detail of every government project, and since he cannot be expected to abandon his own job and do the job of other government officials on the government pay role, we would recommend that failure to execute government programmes and directives, particularly those that effect the welfare of the masses, should be met with severe disciplinary measures.

Sam- Nuvala Fonkem

20

Cameroon Report 15/4/1984: April 6 Coup Attempt: An Appraisal

Introduction: *In today's special program on the abortive coup of April 6th Fai Henry Fonye makes an appraisal of the incident, highlighting the lessons to the learnt from it. History, he says, repeated itself in Cameroon on April 6th. He compares the Republican Guards to the Praetorian Guards of the Roman Empire, established as a special unit for the protection of the emperors. The guards ended up using their military power to overthrow the emperors and to control the Roman Senate's election of successive emperors. Fai Henry Fonye begins by reflecting on the rebels' justification for the coup attempt:*

On April 6th, the Republican Guards launched a coup in Cameroon and came within a hair's breadth of succeeding, but for our gallant and loyal soldiers. Their excuses were unfounded. They falsely cried that under President Paul Biya, human rights were not respected, that the recent trials of the August coup plotters were merely a parody of justice, that the constitution was played upon freely, and that the government and its agents were shot into the higher positions of the ruling structure.

No one needs to dwell on such blatant lies. Cameroonians are not going to be led by any given region; teleguided and master minded by a "psychedelic shack" on the run, trumpeting from abroad like a toothless full dog.

However, the coup attempt has its significance. We Cameroonians have taken peace for granted and unity as noise by politicians for a long time. We now certainly know the value of peace and should be prepared to pay the price, which is eternal vigilance and unabashed commitment to the nation.

Our gallant soldiers have given us the example and the important lesson that in general, the common military training and socializing experiences do breakdown the soldiers' regional attachments concomitantly instilling secular and national attitudes. They proved that military training helps turn soldiers into cohesive entities with a strong national consciousness and that the military units can serve as melting pots in which soldiers tend to lose their tribal characteristics and, as professional managers of force and violence, they did their best and deserve praise.

This lesson is important because, as a reality, all countries in Africa are divided along communal lines, inherited attributes of religion, region, language and ethnicity which sharply distinguish one part of the population from another and thus give rise to intense conflicts. And this is what Mr Ahidjo is exploiting from his hide-outs abroad, and financing with money he allegedly took away from here.

When this commentator appraised President Paul Biya's clemency to the criminals of the famous plot to exterminate his life in August last year, he said that President Paul Biya's action was only a sign of the dawn of the day and not sun shine itself. It happened that even that gesture which gave cause for much reflection and discussion in Cameroon was not appreciated. The mass media and the people of Cameroon did ask for an immediate clean up. Let people be put where they belong. Politics and religion constitute an ideal, the achievement of which should not be too costly. As our colleague of the "Cameroon Tribune" – Shey Mabu has rightly put it, our political elite must gird their loins and clean up promptly for the interest of the populace. To procrastinate on this matter is to lay the foundation for future offence or to put the dice into the box for another throw. Surely we don't want to wear clothes tailored by blacksmiths.

While we remain vigilant and ready to defend our country, let justice take its course now, so that the culprits undergo such an affliction as will give the virtuous Cameroonians a comfortable sense of their immunity, added to that of their worth.

Fai Henry Fonye

Cameroon Report 15/4/1984: In the Dawn of the Abortive Coup

Still within the context of special program on the April 6 coup attempt, Sam-Nuvala Fonkem hails the role of the Armed Forces in quelling the rebellion:

Peace loving Cameroonians would like to congratulate the Armed Forces for their solidarity and action in suppressing the coup attempt. This they accomplished despite material handicap and inferior weapons compared to those manipulated by the rebel forces.

Congratulation also goes to all Cameroonians who in one way or the other helped in neutralising the rebels at the risk of their lives. Some members of the Force are now working overtime and we call on them to bear the burden in good spirit, hoping that those of them involved in the present hardship would be duly rewarded.

In as much as we congratulate the Armed Forces for their part in suppressing the coup attempt, we have every reason to demand that some of them be cautioned with regard to their attitude towards members of the public and property.

There is no doubt that members of the public have been cooperating amicably with the forces of law and order. There is also no doubt that the task of the forces of law and order in the wake of the coup attempt has become tougher than before and that under psychological pressure they are inclined to be nervous.

It would suffice to say that there is need to maintain a healthy and amicable relation between the forces and the public, all of whom are called upon to be more vigilant. This vigilance can only be encouraged dif those who unmask dangerous elements in the society are guaranteed safety and anonymity. This also implies that vigilance should not be used as a means of spreading false reports and settling personal accounts.

Reports should be followed by thorough investigations, void of physical harassment. A word to the wise is sufficient.

Sam- Nuvala Fonkem

22

Cameroon Report 21/5/1984: Reflection on May 20

The act of mediation may assume various postures, moods and objectives, but it all seems to lead to a conscious effort to achieve a better and deeper understanding of the human condition and the universe at large.

Mediation may seek to accommodate the mind to a situation which it cannot control; it may unfortunately turn out not only to be a means of accommodating self-resignation but a pseudo-religious form of escapism.

Mediation as an act of positive thinking however requires that after having ruminated and prayed earnestly to the Gods of the Land for protection against our enemies, we must at the same time engage in a critical self-examination in order to achieve a clearer vision of what is at stake.

The New Deal Administration, endorsed by the unanimous vote of January 1984, emerged from the dark horizon of political and economic stagnation, promising a brighter and more confident future for the nation. Granted that the New Deal package carried many more promises than it has delivered, it was not confidence nor conviction that it lacked. The New Deal could not be said to have been too ambitious, if a few individuals had decided to cooperate with it.

Sincere cooperation is what the New Deal asked for; nothing more. It had counted on every Cameroonian for this cooperation, but then we had also relied on certain political incumbents whose continued presence in the running of public business symbolised everything that stood against the aspirations of the New Deal Administration.

The moment of truth was revealed in the betrayal of April 6th this year, when army mutineers attempted a coup d'état.

After the April 6th events, Cameroonians are all convinced that the country does not need another cataclysm to remind it of the past and to make it see the path the future must take.

The President has appealed for confidence and we believe this confidence has been considerably restored.

It can only be consolidated if the public business doubles its pace and catches up with time already lost.

Sam-Nuvala Fonkem

23

Cameroon Report 9/6/1984: Parastatal Corporations Revisited

Introduction: *After having acknowledged that state corporations have been grossly mismanaged and incurred grave losses and deficits during the past years, it is now time to carry out a blunt analysis of their paralysis and apply swift reforms.* SAM-NUVALA FONKEM *examines parastatal corporations and suggests that immediate action be taken to awaken them to their role:*

We must admit that any sluggish approach to the ailments of state corporations in the name of gradualism would very likely lead the economy to very serious difficulties that may become too chronic to be cured.

When the President of the National Assembly declared that subventions to parastatals should be the exception rather than the rule and that parastatals ought to become more viable and profitable, he was merely echoing and confirming public suspicion that public corporations, in the previous administration, had been set up as vehicles for the self-enrichment of political comrades and cronies.

A diagnosis of the problem of parastatals indicates that their failure can be attributed to structural deficiencies and mismanagement. The mismanagement was possible through the lack of clarity in the definition of government investments in statutory corporations.

It is common knowledge for example that corporation bosses wielded immense authority and influence over the government departments under whose authority they had been placed.

A 1980 official report of the National Investment Corporation, SNI, the holding company through which government acquires shares in both parastatals and private ventures, indicates that the corporation has not been able to fulfil its objectives largely as a result of its imprecise authority in relation to statutory corporations.

The report stated that SNI's financial operations were in a mess not because of inefficient internal management, but as a result of huge deficits incurred by parastatals and companies in which it holds shares. Its loan operations have not been fruitful as well. As of June 1980, CFA 9.8 billion francs representing 83% of SNI's loans went to CAMSUCO, STPC, CERICAM, and COCAM, all of them white elephants, which ran combined losses of 4.6 billion francs. No one doubts that such an economic performance is not only catastrophic, but also prophetic.

Although the SNI appears to be only one out of several vehicles through which government investments are channelled, it seems to lack the supervisory authority by which it can redress the financial situation of its affiliates which are unfortunately running heavy deficits.

The holding company may have a direct inspection of the books of statutory corporations but lacks the authority to control their financial operations owing to lack of definition of authority and the conflict of authority that necessarily arises between the investment company and the management executive of parastatals.

Further investments have been held up as a result of accrued deficits, the clearing of these deficits and the bolstering of the capital of shaky enterprises.

The procedure for signing contracts and the relation between government departments and parastatals on one hand and the investment corporation on the other hand, are said to be placed under a complex network of influence and pressure from various quarters, giving rise to contradictions and conflicts of interest.

If this analysis has focused lengthily on the investment corporation it is because we feel the restructuring and reorganisation of the objectives and authority of this body constitutes one of the most rational solutions to the mismanagement problems faced by statutory corporations. Of course, we also believe that the reorganisation of the statutory corporations themselves and an objective exercise aimed at identifying the unsuccessful aspects of their operations are equally necessary to safeguard government investment and make them become more profitable.

The recent reorganisation of some major parastatals should not stop at merely changing their General Managers. The General Managers who led their corporations to bankruptcy did not succeed in doing so single-handedly. Replacements in the lower executive ranks are imperative and should preserve the new spirit of merit and competence, not favouritism as a means of rewarding the specially privileged protégés of political nonentities.

The new rule that subventions to parastatals should be the exception rather than the rule should be immediately applied. Erratic and ill-considered subventions to poorly managed corporations have also been largely responsible for the encouragement of laxity and mismanagement in these organisations. If mismanagement is not seriously checked, and we believe the government is bent on checking it this time, the country may one day find itself in the ranks of the very Least Developed and face the prospect of being blacklisted in the world community as insolvent.

Sam-Nuvala Fonkem

24

Cameroon Report 01/1/1985, Chasing Files: A Product of Centralisation

Introduction: *Over the week, there were a series of ceremonies organised to present New Year wishes to members of government by the staff of various ministries. Most remarkable among the statements made by the Ministers, were those by Trade and Industry Minister, and that of Planning and Regional Development Messrs NOMO ONGOLO and YOUSSOUFA DAOUDA who called on officials to delegate powers where necessary so as to speed-up the processing of files. This meant resurrecting the issue of "chasing files". News commentator, SAM- NUVALA FONKEM terms it a dead issue but says its solution could only be found in real decentralisation:*

Responding to New Year wishes presented by officials of their respective departments, the Trade and Industry Minister and the Minister of Planning and Regional Development resurrected a seemingly dead issue, the eradication of which was emphatically stated in President BIYA'S Bamenda declaration in February 1983 to put an end to the question of chasing files.

The costly business of "chasing files" may be termed a dead issue since, as it would appear, nothing can be done about it. The public has come to accept it as a necessary evil and condoned its inconveniences and wastefulness as a standard feature of our underdevelopment. The practice of chasing files has even become a touristic vocation for some and a pilgrimage for others, all depending on your frame of mind.

The attractions of file-chasing have become so pervasive that like an insatiable gambler, civil servants are not even deterred by the prospects of spending 100.000 francs to undertake a bureaucratic pilgrimage to Yaounde for the purpose of chasing emoluments hardly worth 10.000 francs. Of course, the civil servant has a right to protect his interest, but alas, at what cost? It would be quite a useful study for experts to work out government losses in man power and output resulting from time lost in the wild-goose chase.

Government and the people believe and agreed that the solution to the problem is decentralisation and measures to achieve this goal have notably been applied in the Public Service Ministry. This structural expansion which entails a willingness to delegate powers has truly been inculcated in the system. What could be the level of willingness among those who have vested interest in the file-chasing enterprise? It should not be surprising to describe the practice as an enterprise, as one cynic noted, adding perspicaciously that decentralising the administration would also mean decentralising the bribe-taking syndicate, a factor that may partially explain the reluctance to share any kind of position or power that fetches illegal gains.

Apart from vested interest, the practice of centralisation as a feature of emerging nation states concerned with nationalistic ambitions of total mobilisation has unfortunately produced a certain power jealousy and drunkenness that has blinded its actors against the very principles of a civil service. The Civil Service is first of all a service to the public and secondly it has got to be civil. What one observes, however, is that some people have given it the stamp of discourtesy and disservice.

In trying to reform the apparently irredeemable bureaucratic system, we would have to rely a great deal on the policy of moralisation and define its implications with regard to administrative inefficiency and indiscipline. What, for example, should be done if an administrator is shown to have been sitting on somebody's file or conjured it into thin air? For how long must a file be sat upon before it lays an egg? Do the various government departments have a standard flow chart for processing files and is there a checking system to detect obstacles along the chain process?

Government departments particularly the Public Service, Finance and Education which deal with large numbers of people should produce manuals on the salient features of their activities and what the public ought to know about their functioning. Government departments have to get out of their habitual lethargy and join the information campaign being waged in other sectors of national life. The price of ignorance is too high and the education of the public should be taken more seriously than ever before.

The best of our decentralisation process lies in the amount of power we are willing to delegate to provincial and local authorities and the establishment of an efficient communications link between the delegations and the central administration.

Sam- Nuvala Fonkem

Cameroon Report 20/01/85: The Plight of our Farmers

Introduction: *It has become a regular theme for sermons that farmers hold the live-wire of the Cameroonian economy. But while non-farmers maintain the highest standards of living in this country, these farmers have remained the subsistence- level citizens. They have barely enough to send a few children to school, prepare for feasts like Christmas and keep a bit for beer and a grass-roof house. While blaming the world division of labour which has forced the prices of agricultural products to be very low compared to those of manufactured goods, those nationals who have been made rich by being asked to deal with agricultural cooperatives bear heavy responsibility. Newsman AKWANKA JOE NDIFOR looks at the problems of our farmers as another coffee season begins in the country:*

It is more than two years now that Cameroon Report first brought to the knowledge of the public the famous North West Cooperative scandal. This was when the administration had realized the gross and unpardonable misuse of poor farmers' monies by a handful of unscrupulous individuals and decided to dissolve the body.

Although one of our reporters almost got lynched when he first made a commentary on the issue, this programme decided to take sides with the government in protecting the interests of our famers who today are the live-wire of Cameroon's economy. Other smaller cooperatives were examined and the same criminal activities were uncovered, although it is not yet clear whether those responsible were punished in conformity with public opinion.

It is equally unclear whether the wind that swept the North West Cooperative Union also affected other parts of the country.

In spite of all these steps taken by the administration to check those vices, it would appear things never worked. This is confirmed by the shocking disclosure by the Minister of Trade and Industry last week that the production of Robusta coffee dropped by 55 % and Arabica coffee by 26 %. Now this is a clear indication that much still has to be done to recapture waning interest of our farmers in agriculture.

Anybody who cares about the well being of our farmers will agree with this reporter that the New Deal government has been doing much of late to win back the confidence of the farmer. The National Agro-pastoral Show in Bamenda is one of the examples. Competitions for the best farms are being organised all over the country. The National Fund for Rural Development (FONADER) has been decentralized which gives us hope that it will henceforth be a true farmers' bank and not the personal property of any individual.

In spite of the recent increase in the prices of coffee and cocoa by the Head of State, the National Produce Marketing Board has been running a campaign promising farmers bonuses for the produce they sell. On top of all, last week, the Minister of Trade and Industry announced that even commercial banks will henceforth be prepared to give loans to farmers. These are all excellent decisions which leave us with the feeling that Cameroonian farmers may be in heaven by next week.

We first got the impression under the former regime that farmers were unhappy when a story was making the rounds about a certain man who left his village to town and when he was shown a skyscraper of a cooperative building, he went back home and in anger, decided to cut down his coffee plants to cultivate plantains in their place. We are not saying that he was right in doing so. But one question remains: What forced him to take such a decision?

Now take a ride at night, say from Bamenda to Bafoussam. You will come across a handful of road-blocks not manned by the forces of law and order but by cooperative officials. Their aim? To check illegal dealings in the sale of coffee. Why this smuggling? Because there is little or no confidence in the cooperative organisation.

In fact, the warning by the Ministry of Trade and Industry to those who deal with cash crops that they would be severely punished if their activities were irregular comes at the appropriate moment. We cannot deny the fact that the degree of lawlessness is still so high in this country that there are people or better still outlaws who feel that the law is helpless before them. Such individuals are also in the fabric of cash crop dealings in the country and such a warning was clearly directed at them.

We tried to hide behind the cloak of drought to say it alone was responsible for the sharp decline in coffee production. It may have been just one of the factors. There are others which are equally important. Farmers present their crops but the money is only received after very long delays as if the farmer has no responsibilities. The result is that farmers prefer to grow food crops which they could sell and get the cash on the spot.

In spite of fluctuations in the prices of raw material in the world market, which have continued to have an adverse effect on the nation's economy, we cannot deny the fact that there are still many outlaws in the sale of these commodities still making their large stomachs longer through financial irregularities.

These are people who will drive their ill-gotten cars, splash mud on the very farmer from whom they stole the money, without as much as giving a look.

While we all look up to the administration to look for such people and have them severely punished, we also appeal to our farmers to continue the good job they have been doing. Things have been rough so far but there are clear indications that a solution to their problems is around the corner.

Akwanka Joe Ndifor

Cameroon Report 22/4/85: The One-shift and Two-shift Working systems

Introduction: *As the ZAMBO Commission continued its mission today, the population has asked for a one-shift working system as a more appropriate way of implementing stringency at work. EBSSIY NGUM now examines the merits and demerits of the one-shift and two-shift working systems in Cameroon:*

The two-shift working system is heavier on workers, thus bringing about a lazy attitude towards work and finally making the administrative machinery less efficient.

In the one-shift system west of the Mungo, the day is shared between office work and other private activities which could include farming, house work, studying, playing, visits and drinking. In this case it is easier for the authorities to control the movement of workers during working hours.

In the two-shift system, the whole day is virtually taken up by work even if it is not done. This is because psychologically, people know that within the week it is difficult to do any other thing. So in the morning, people are slow to start. Consequently most workers enter their offices from 9.30 am and by II am, they want to go home and cook, eat, drink, and take siesta. Most of these people end their siesta at 3 pm, feeling more tired than they were before it.

They get ready to go back to work by 3.30 pm and settle down to work at 4 pm. By 5 pm everybody is itching to go home because the day has been too busy. Finally, only about

2 ½ hours are put into effective work for those who do not drink during break time.

On the other hand, in the one-shift system, most people do not feel taxed by work. By 8 am most people are in their offices and work is done up to 2 pm. In this system, the lazy habit of taking siesta is discouraged; therefore, about six hours are effectively put into work.

When one looks at the financial burdens of the two systems, one notices that a worker in the two-shift system spends at least 8.800 francs CFA a month on taxi, while the one shift worker spends only 4.800 francs. The two-shift working housewife hardly goes to work a Saturdays because she sees it as the only opportunity to go shopping and keep the home clean. Her one-shift working counterpart has 3 ½ hours of free daylight time every day.

By month end, most workers in the two-shift system can no longer afford going to work twice because of poverty and the offices become empty in the afternoons.

The other reasons workers are militating for a one-shift working system are also understandable because in the first place, there is no time for promoting the Green Revolution. The whole day is occupied and people do not have time to manage farms. This situation leaves agriculture mainly in the hands of peasants who cannot go beyond mere subsistence farming.

In the second place, the two-shift system looks like a barrier to further studies. At the end of the day, people are so worn out that they can no longer pick up any book to read and their working knowledge is not renewed. Thirdly, the two-shift working system has engendered the two shift schooling system. The children spend the whole day under school care and do not have time for private studies or research.

Worse still, they are deprived of parental care because they meet their parents only at night when little can be learnt. The children consequently learn only unruly behaviour along the road from home to school and back.

Ebssiy Ngum

Cameroon Report 25/4/1985: Decentralisation versus Decongestion

Introduction: *As the ZAMBO Commission continued its nation-wide safari, there has been a recurrence of the request for greater decentralization of the administration. This falls in line with the regular pronouncements on bringing the administration nearer the people. EBSSIY NGUM examines the importance of decentralisation by way of definition:*

Does the multiplication of ministerial posts, the creation of many provincial services and the creation of more provinces mean decentralisation No! It means de-concentration.

Now that militants and workers in Bamenda, Buea and other places are asking for greater decentralisation of the administrative machinery, it is important that people know what they are asking for.

De-concentration is an offshoot of centralisation and leaves decision making only to central authorities. In other words, the multiplication of authorities down the line is only a way of ensuring greater control and creating posts. In this case a provincial authority cannot take any decision that has a financial or economic incidence, except by following instructions from central authorities.

Evidence of this is seen in the fact that the creation of more provinces, the extension of the Ministry of Public Service to the provinces, and the re-organisation of ministries to allow for more departments and services, have not solved the problem of chasing files.

It is also common place that when the Governor undertakes a meet-the-people's tour, he listens to the people's complaints about administrative facilities, economic infrastructure and academic institutions, but tells them that he will transmit their problems to the competent authorities.

Such authorities are so far away that even such complaints reach them, they do not feel the impact at all. And the replies hardly ever come.

Decentralisation means that local leaders come from the bottom, they enjoy wide power, the centre has little control over them and fundamental decisions are taken by them. In such a situation, a governor for instance, will be a leader, capable of solving economic and financial problems at the level of the province without seeking instructions from elsewhere. He will be a people's leader answerable to them and sensitive to their problems.

People's files will then be kept at provincial level and not at national level if they are serving the provincial administration. Those serving the national administration will have their files kept in the national headquarters. This will certainly mean bringing the people nearer the administration.

It is therefore hoped that when militants are asking for greater decentralisation, they do not mean the creation of more administrative units and provincial services, or more ministerial posts because that will not amount to what they are complaining about.

They should be thinking of ways to give provincial authorities greater autonomy through decentralizing the computer service, and making the provincial administration take care of development at provincial level.

Ebssiy Ngum

28

Cameroon Report 15/5/1985: 13th Anniversary of the Unitary State

British superstition has it that the number 13 is an unlucky number, but 13 in the case of the age of the unitary state signifies that it has attained adolescence, an adolescence which hopefully would blossom to a ripe maturity.

Since the creation o the unitary state in 1972, the nation has made significant strides in development, a development that has seen an expansion of socio-economic and communications infrastructures and earned Cameroon the status of the bread basket of the Central Africa sub region.

Although food self-sufficiency has been attained, particularly at a period of widespread famine in the continent, much still has to be done to improve the production sector with regard to finished and semi-finished products which is the task of a number of government agencies and parastatal corporations, the majority of which have become a liability rather than an asset to the state.

A glaring aspect which has to be tackled is the bridging of the wide gap between the rich and the poor and instituting a more rational system of distributing remunerations and the wealth of the nation. The state has still to establish rational criteria for the assessment and distribution of sacrifices and benefits on a regional basis. Although the country has gone on record for its healthy 6.5% annual economic growth, behind this figure is a catalogue of socio-economic malpractices, corruption and graft, the eradication of which the government has still to draw up a blueprint.

On the social aspect, the most disturbing issue remains the application of bilingualism at all levels of public life – in the educational system, the administration and the public and private sectors.

The application of bilingualism, officially upheld as an inevitable factor of the reunification of the country, leaves much to be desired and has sparked off complaints from the English speaking communities which are deprived of benefiting from official and general information much of which is published in French. Thirteen years after the setting up of the unitary state, Government departments still publish news handouts only in French and a look at all the parastatals which function without translators gives the impression that they are above government policy. It is certainly not government policy to deprive any given community because of a language handicap, but the indifference shown towards the policy of bilingualism should be denounced and corrected more forcefully than ever before.

The over-centralisation of the Administration still remains a constant headache and it is hoped that the Zambo commission which has been on a nation-wide fact-finding mission will come up with speedy solutions.

Politically the unitary state has made considerable mileage though not without wear and tear as well as breakdowns such as the 1983 August coup plot and the 1984 April 6th coup attempt which temporarily brought the state to a standstill, a slowdown which the leader of the New Deal turned into a political asset, enabling him to get rid of some old political barons.

Recent political changes include the change of political precepts and the legitimation of political norms as well as a ritual of baptism that saw the modification of the denomination of the state from the United Republic of Cameroon to simply the Republic of Cameroon and the change of the name of the party from the Cameroon National Union to the Cameroon People's Democratic Movement.

These name changes have been given several official interpretations. The modification of the name of the country was said to have been aimed at dispelling the notion that the country was made up of several states while the change of party name was aimed at giving a new lease of life to the party and emphasising to the nation that the party, under the New Deal, encompassed all shades of political opinion. A change of name could possibly bring about a change of mentality and attitude, but for this to be achieved, concrete and convincing programs must be embarked upon to give meaning to name changes or else one may tend to ask the old question – after all what's in a name?

The most significant political change since the unitary state was set up in 1972, in this reporter's opinion, has been the stepping down of the former president and the emergence of Mr. Biya who incarnates the nation's hope for open and genuine democracy and who has declared his intention to move the country from national unity to national integration.

Such an ambitious plan can only be achieved through sacrifices and such sacrifices should be evenly and equitably distributed to avoid public anxiety, discontent, and disappointment.

Thirteen years is not much, but then it is not insignificant. In as much as youth is not a virtue as some old political guards have insisted, we must reckon with the fact that wisdom is not the prerogative of old age. Thus, 13 years of a unitary state can form a solid base for greater political achievements if only such achievements do not entail discriminatory and undue deprivation of certain areas of the country.

Sam-Nuvala Fonkem

29

Cameroon Report 25/5/1985: The Role of Development Committees

Ever since provincial development committees became institutionalised in 1977, observers have always been at a loss when it comes to assessing their impact on the elaboration of the national five-year development plans.

Given that 5-Year Development plans are mere plans, as it were, and that several pertinent objectives are hardly realised by their term of expiration, one must regard them as sheer statements of good intention. These statements of good intention, so to speak, provide the framework for development committees, whereas one would expect such a framework to reflect the expressed needs or development priorities of the various local communities as suggested by them and not dictated by some elusive and faceless bureaucratic process which may end up by misunderstanding the needs of local communities. This would also allow for a more democratic participation of the population in policy making-running from the bottom to the top (although the bottom has recently and unfortunately become officially indentified with falsehood and rumour mongering).

Although private initiative has always been propounded as a complimentary policy to what is officially referred to as self-reliant development (which one learned professor at Yaounde University describes as a misnomer that should read 'self-help'), self-reliant development and local private initiative have had only a marginal impact on the socio-economic life of certain areas of the country. Reasons include the complicated bureaucratic process and conditions for attracting local and foreign private capital, the selfishness of holders of local private capital resources and their unwillingness to go into more serious and creative areas of production, their tendency to restrict themselves to the role of middle-men or what is locally known as 'buy- am- sell-am' or better still the quick profit-short term risk ventures, thereby neglecting certain vital areas of production.

Other factors affecting self-reliant development include the concentration of industrial activity in only certain areas defined as industrial zones and even when such activity is extended to more remote areas, as it is rarely the case, it has failed to have any significant effect on the economic life of the local population in terms of social investment projects, the hiring and training of local manpower and profit sharing.

This point brings to mind the classical incident in Francis Bebey's novel "Agatha Moudio's Son" in which the local population, in an unexpected moment of enlightenment, challenged a group of white colonialists whose hunting sprees were almost depleting the wildlife population. They rightly considered that the continued plundering of their wildlife without compensation was tantamount to plundering a vital sector of their patrimony. If our economic planners could borrow a bit of wisdom form the philosophy of that pre-independence rural community, then it would be possible to avoid social injustice in the mobilisation and reallocation of revenue.

Talking about the mobilisation and reallocation of revenue, one observes a certain policy by industrial firms operating outside the traditional zones of industrial activity to show indifference towards the economic growth of the local areas they exploit. A case that readily comes to mind is the recently inaugurated mineral water factory at Mile 29 in Fako Division, a factory which our correspondent said has its headquarters in the commercial capital of Douala, Wouri division and thus pays its company, turnover and profit taxes in Douala and not at Mile 29.

If the above deduction is true of the mineral water factory (and I am told it is true of yet another, the biggest industrial concern in Fako Division) then one has to ask if our Inland Revenue policy does not need some serious revision.

It would seem that although government is doing everything to encourage the expansion of industries to the countryside by providing some tax incentives, the application of these innovations leaves much to be desired in terms of actual economic impact on the local areas under exploitation. Hence, self-reliant development as a policy has come to provide more food for thought than food for the stomach particularly as the means for generating local revenue is either absent or manipulated to serve individual interests.

All this is not intended to show that development plans are useless. On the contrary, they form the concrete aspect of orderly planning which is indispensable for all governments. All that is being meant here is that the drawing up of these plans requires more rational and pragmatic considerations as well as a genuine spirit of social justice and human dignity.

Sam-Nuvala Fonkem

Cameroon Report 01/6/1985: 1985 Budgetary Session

On the eve of the annual budgetary session of our honourable members of parliament, it is only fitting to salute them in advance of their difficult task of sharing the national cake amongst highly competing needs and interests.

Cameroonians are proud to note the substantial increases in the national budget by an average of 100 billion francs a year since President Biya come to power and also proud to know that the budget is entirely financed from internal resources. Somehow the majority of the people still have misgivings and are still suspicious about the deployment of the Special Budget largely made up of oil revenues, the amount of which is still kept beyond the control of parliament. Suspicion does not arise from any proof that it is being misused, since the President himself informed the nation through the foreign press that the current investment budget of 220 billion was given an additional boost of 150 billion from the Special Budget. Misgivings arise from the fact that shrouding oil revenues from parliamentary scrutiny does not entirely satisfy hopes for public accountability.

The budgetary session begins holding amidst complains that some suppliers' bills have not been paid and may not be paid before the new finance bill under study goes into effect. The session will be meeting amidst traditional complains of lack of necessary equipment in government departments that were supposed to have been bought during the fiscal year just ending. The session will be holding amidst the traditional last minute helter-skelter by purchasing departments seeking ghost suppliers to furnish fictitious bills for equipment that were never and will never be delivered.

These practices are not unknown and it is left to our MPs not only to decide on the various ministerial budgetary allocations but also to seek ways to end such practices.

True enough, parliament's major task this session, as it is usually the case, is to concentrate on the budget; nevertheless the public expects other important, if not pleasant surprises, within the framework of the New Deal's commitment to democratise the institutions of the state. Many people expected too much from the Bamenda Congress concerning the democratisation of the electoral system as a whole, but some analysts thought that in not making any definitive statements in that line in Bamenda, the President was merely emphasising the separation of the party from the state and that party occasions should deal with party issues while state occasions should deal with state matters.

It is everyone's hope that parliament comes up with pleasant surprises apart from an increase in budgetary allocations which should be a foregone conclusion for a country with an economic growth rate that is on international record for being the best in black Africa.

Sam-Nuvala Fonkem

Cameroon Report 30/6/1985: MUNA on Bilingualism

Introduction: *Closing this year's budgetary session of Parliament, House Speaker, Hon. S. T. MUNA said that the "National Assembly was practising an acceptable level of bilingualism even if Cameroon Report disagrees with him." For the sake of clarity and to avoid rumour-mongering, Julius Wamey re-examines the question of bilingualism as raised by Hon. Muna:*

To start with, we were rather pleased and flattered to hear that the Speaker of the Assembly, Hon. S. T. Muna listens to Cameroon Report and could admit it in a plenary session of parliament. But at the risk of seeming to dispute the Honourable Speaker, I would like to make some observations.

Our policy of bilingualism was enshrined into the constitution by the Federal Assembly almost a quarter of a century ago. Quite a good number of our present parliamentarians were in that Federal Assembly. Few of them are hardly any more bilingual than they were twenty-five years ago.

Allowance can be made for those advanced in age and the modest level of education of most assembly men but it would be outrageous to expect forgiveness for parliament's neglect of the policy of bilingualism.

Let me explain this further. In most bilingual countries, there is usually a public body, such as an ombudsman, responsible for the enforcement and application of legislation on language. Such bodies usually strive to protect the language rights of minorities. Here, no such thing exists. Our representatives carelessly left the application of this excellent policy to the dubious goodwill of the civil service, the academic system and an unsuspecting citizenry.

When the Honourable Speaker talks of the existence of "an acceptable level of bilingualism" in the National Assembly, one cannot help but be disagreeably surprised. One would automatically assume that the very body that decided we should be bilingual should use both languages in a routine manner without expecting praise for it, or praising itself either. It is about the same as a dutiful child boasting that it fetched water for the mother.

The announcement that parliament would be opening a centre for the promotion of bilingualism is a laudable one even if it comes twenty-five years late. This is an example to be emulated. In fact, parliament could itself initiate legislation to make the setting up of such centres mandatory countrywide.

We are in entire agreement with Honourable Muna that bilingualism is a national option and not an Anglophone or francophone affair. We might add, with good reason that is not, or should not be, an Anglophone affair. I say this with good reason because in the newsroom we are painfully aware daily of the frustrations attendant on working in a second language.

Anglophone journalists are expected to be able to translate official texts replete with technical terms and bureaucratic jargon and all this at a speed a professional translator cannot sustain. Any errors resulting from this complex and hasty job are promptly laid at the poor journalist's door.

Is it excusable that President Paul Biya, Speaker S. T. Muna and a good number of Ministers should be able to express themselves fluently in both official languages, at their age, while a young graduate from ENAM or the University cannot sustain a brief conversation in his office in a second official language? This is not excusable.

If by pointing out these deficiencies, Cameroon Report is perceived as being negative and discouraging in its criticism, then we would like to know what constructive criticism is all about.

We have often been accused of being destructive, negative and even subversive in our commentaries by officials who find our criticisms hitting too close to home. However, in this instance, the Speaker of our parliament is talking on behalf of his colleagues, since he has himself made the greatest efforts to become bilingual.

Is it wrong if we demand that younger men than Mr. Muna make the same effort? We shall stop criticising shortcomings in public life when we are told to do so but until then, we were trained to know that we are the watchdogs of society.

All we want to do is to see that laws passed by our parliament and policies drawn up by our government are not ridiculed by its own agents.

Julius Wamey

Cameroon Report 14/7/1985: The Concept of Development Journalism

The role of the press in under-developed countries has remained controversial. It has even been made demanding by the duty given to it by the necessities of development. That is why there is the talk of development journalism in developing countries. Yet, this concept has not yet been understood, even by professionals.

First of all, development means the creation of goods and services, and not their consumption. Consequently, development journalism should mean journalism that promotes the creation of goods and services.

Journalists are not factory workers, neither are they engineers to invent and manufacture goods, not even taxi drivers to render services to people. It therefore means that the journalist can only serve either as an alarm to wake people up, or as watch-dog of society to make sure that people play their roles well, which will consequently lead to the creation of better goods and services. This certainly amounts to development.

But many people are still missing the point. Even the press in the most developed countries has not yet been reduced to praise-singing choral groups. This is because no matter the level of development, an effort is still required to sustain it, and people have to remain awake to avoid retrogression.

This situation ought to be understood more by under-developed countries, Cameroon being no exception, because they are victims of oppression from the world's economic giants. They are suffering from laziness, poor organization that enables people in offices to steal public funds as if it were a legal duty. Nobody seems to know the importance of his own role even in a service; a service head cares only for his duty allowance and free lodging, and a clerk serves only his director and not the public.

Should a state-owned newspaper or radio-television station stay mute in the face of these evils or backwardness under the pretext that it is practising development journalism? Then there will be no basis for a state at all. Nobody will pay taxes to sponsor presidents, ministers and general managers when they are not working for him.

This programme believes that there is a way out of under-development. That is why it seeks to awaken everybody, from top to bottom, so as to stimulate the creation of goods and services. Some people will disagree, but we all know that under-development came about as a historical necessity and not as a historical alternative.

Be sure that we will continue to fight under-development in our own way.

Ebssiy Ngum

33

Cameroon Report 08/8/1985: The Question of Certificate Equivalence

The practice of equating academic and professional qualifications obtained abroad is not unusual and useless as it may seem, but the practice becomes repugnant when it is used as an instrument of social disequilibrium.

Differences in the country's two educational systems warrant that students seeking higher education abroad either go to French-speaking or Anglo-Saxon institutions as well as others, but the various stages of ascendency remain very much the same. The stages include a first degree, a post graduate diploma, a master's degree and a doctorate.

The acquisition of the doctorate varies from 5-10 years after a first degree, depending on the student's capabilities and the work load of the programme. Somehow there is a persistent belief in Cameroon that post graduate qualifications from French-speaking institutions are superior to those from Anglo-Saxon establishments ostensibly because of differences in duration, a criterion which has a much lesser value than content and scope of educational programmes. Hence it has regrettably become normal for a holder of a French doctorate to be recruited on a higher salary scale than his counterpart from an Anglo-Saxon University. This applies at all levels of post graduate recruitment in both the public and private sectors.

Although the labour code is clear on this matter, holders of Anglo-Saxon degrees obtained abroad are invariably relegated to one or two salary scales below their counterparts from French-speaking institutions. (Except a few who are able to obtain effective political intervention).

There has been a general acquiescence with regard to this practice for reasons which cannot be explained without acknowledging the prevalence of a superiority complex derived from numerical superiority and not qualitative assessment. The institution of certificate equivalence is not merely aimed at assessing qualifications but has been perversely used as an instrument of reclassifying certain people to the lower rungs of the job market and instilling in them a sense of professional inadequacy which cannot be justified. It would be recalled that this same attitude was mainly responsible for what became known as the G.C.E. crisis which up till now has not been resolved and can only be resolved by respecting the cultural diversity of the country, a diversity which should be considered an asset, not a liability.

It should be noted, however, that attempts to devalue academic and professional qualifications from Anglo-Saxon institutions by means of a biased bureaucratic machinery does not in any way reduce the intrinsic value of these qualifications. The extrinsic values attached to them by this machinery only foster the undesirable sentiments of disappointment, de-motivation, rustication, estrangement and brain drain. This situation, compounded with many other discriminatory practices, does not speak well of national objectives to exercise social justice, maintain social balance and respect cultural values. Thus practices likely to jeopardize the stability of the country such as these should not be treated in an expedient manner, as it is the case, but with the profound perception and assessment of intrinsic cultural values.

The delay tactics involved in the procedure for obtaining certificate equivalence does not favour Anglophones seeking equivalence in the prevalent rat race in the labour market. This procedure could be said to be unnecessarily time consuming, considering that these Anglo-Saxon qualifications are not unknown to the authorities.

Sam-Nuvala Fonkem

34

Cameroon Report 18/8/1985: Harmonising Our Two Legal Systems

The Minister of State for Justice and Keeper of the Seals is reported to have castigated magistrates in the North West and South West provinces for violation, contempt and ignorance of the law. The charge was made during stormy meetings with the magistrates more than a fortnight ago.

Cameroon Tribune reports that in a fourteen-page strongly worded address carrying the tone of a warning, the Minister told the magistrates of the Anglophone provinces that some of them give the impression that they live in a closed circle, in contempt of the statutes which govern them and the laws of the Republic.

Prior to the Minister's visits to those provinces, we were told that he was going there to discuss the implementation of already harmonised legal texts, the content of which he failed to discuss with the professionals.

What is obvious, however, is that the Minister had gone to bully the magistrates to accept the implementation of legislation whose merits are questionable and evidently detrimental to the well-being of the Anglophone provinces.

This deduction is based on the Minister's own observation that "even if this legislation with its innovations goes against some of our convictions, beliefs and customs, it should be rigorously applied by the magistrates."

The Minister does not hide the fact that this so-called harmonised legislation may go against the customs, beliefs and convictions of the Anglophone provinces. He suggests that "the national integration we call for can only be achieved if all the citizens... show proof of good faith in the application of the laws... passed by the National Assembly."

The Minister ignores the recent pronouncement by the Honourable Speaker of the National Assembly that the process of integration should be voluntary. Somehow the Minister believes the process should be dictatorial and compulsory even if it goes against customs and convictions. This approach raises a number of political and philosophical questions related to the formulation and application of laws.

The philosophical question is: should laws be made which are undoubtedly against the customs and welfare of any given community? And is it possible to apply laws without conviction? Furthermore, is it politically wise to apply alien laws in the name of integration? The application of such laws can only bring about alienation which the Minister himself recognises when he talks of some Anglophone magistrates giving the impression of living in a closed circle.

The new criminal procedure code which is at the centre of this debate is supposed to be a harmonised version of the English and French-derived criminal procedures applicable in the Anglophone and francophone sectors of the country. What the public would want to know is why the authorities want to harmonise them in the first place. The Anglo-Saxon code is characterised by its accusatorial approach while the French Napoleonic code is base on the inquisitorial approach to criminal matters.

In very simple terms, the one holds that no one is guilty of a crime until the law proves him to be guilty beyond reasonable doubts, while the other holds, prejudicially though, that one is guilty until he can prove the contrary. The one respects the principle of habeas corpus while the other believes in rampant and indefinite powers of detention and the deprivation of individual rights.

The question Cameroon Report would like to ask the Honourable Keeper of the Seals is what hybrid of a legal system does he expect to achieve when he blends the accusatorial and the inquisitorial principles of criminal procedure? It is true Cameroon is a unique country especially in its recent hectic efforts towards integration, but it should not lose sight of the fact that the country is only unique because of its cultural diversity and to deny that fact is to deny the identity of the country which is far from being a homogenous society.

There are certainly other disturbing elements in the Minister's pronouncements to the magistrates, particularly when he implies that some personalities in the country are above the law and that criminal proceedings against such persons must pass through the chancellery.

In apparent reference to the alleged scandal at the SONARA oil refinery in Limbe, the Minister warned the magistrates against divulging information to the press, a warning which can only be seen as being contrary to the newly-regained press freedom which the New Deal government displays as a show-case of open democracy.

In effect, the Minister's charge against the magistrates has done severe damage to the legal profession in that the credibility and authority of the Anglophone magistrates have been grossly undermined.

We hope that when the so-called harmonised legislation is examined in parliament, political fanaticism should give way to logic and realism.

Sam-Nuvala Fonkem

35

Cameroon Report 06/10/85: The First October Story

Introduction: *After about twelve years of silence, there was renewed talk of 1st October this year. It however ended at the level of news talks with no festivities. As anchorman for Cameroon Report, this is what EBSSIY NGUM had to say on the occasion:*

The story being told in Cameroon today started in 1884 at the Berlin conference when more than two hundred ethnic groups were carved out as a colonial parcel and given to Germany.

Thirty-five years later, another meeting which did not seek our opinion split Cameroon into two so as to satisfy the imperial interests of France and Britain. This separation was in force for forty years and accounts for the fact that Cameroon today combines two foreign cultures which are legacies of the colonial past.

Assimilation on the one hand and indirect rule on the other, have had varying impacts on the affected people. The plurality of our cultural settings and the desire for unity, have forced Cameroonians to cling to their colonial legacies as the only basis for a more accommodating frame of reference. This wider frame has as its only vehicle of expression, English and French —an indication that language is more powerful than a name. What is in a name?

We may equally conclude that colonial rule precipitated the creation of nation-states from the multitude of nationalities, tribes, and ethnic groups. Colonial masters succeeded because they used foreign languages so as to better dominate and uniformise their relations within their areas of jurisdiction.

The evolution, however, has been steady since the great re-union of 1st October, 1961. It was not only a re-union of people, but that of constitutions which recognized the historical past of each main cultural community.

We saw the writing on the wall on 1st September 1966 when the various political parties of the two communities gave up their identities. This was certainly a sign of good-will, yet naive. It turned out that a dictatorship had been ushered in on a gold platter. The no-return move came on May 20th 1972 with the unification of constitutions. The Federal Republic of Cameroon became a United Republic with a clear intention to ignore the historical past of the two main communities though we still have to know whether that intention was concretised. It also reduced both judicial independence and individual freedoms.

The United Republic might have governed Cameroon badly for twelve years but it defended itself well because it lasted and died in peace and in one piece.

General DE GAULLE said that "what separates the men from the boys in politics is that the boys want high offices in order to be somebody, the men want high office in order to do something".

On 6th November 1982, on taking office as second President of the United Republic, PAUL BIYA had a programme known as the New Deal. He might have wanted to distinguish himself from the boys in politics. The intention then was to keep only men in politics so that they can do something to bring about concrete progress, even in institutions.

Many thought it was an end to conservatism, abuse of justice, misuse of power, fraud, tribalism and rule by one man surrounded by his worshippers.

It sounded like the dawn of a new era with much said on freedom of everything except crime as known in common law. Hopes were awakened as people recalled the pre-1966 days when there was competition for public office with everybody given the chance. People have since looked forward to new electoral laws that respect the electorate.

However, the Republic too is defending itself well as the storms either stress unity to ignore diversity, or diversity to ignore unity. The message remains that there is unity in diversity.

Twenty-four years after, Cameroon remains united- an indication that even if original detail was ignored, the global concept of re-unification had a good base because of sacrificial good-will on the part of some participants at the Foumban constitutional conference in 1961.

Cameroon Report however still sees that we are constitutionally united, institutionally in unity, culturally in diversity, linguistically talking bilingualism, socially in the seas, politically under great expectations and everybody still has to be equal before the law as a war against high office crimes.

Finally, good government turns cultural pluralism into an asset and conquers instabilities. Empty rhetoric only escorts boys out of high offices while men stay on the sidelines and watch.

Ebssiy Ngum

Cameroon Report 20/5/1986, May 20th: Our Dream of a New and Great Cameroon

Introduction: *National Day celebration on May 20th this year was marked by exceptional enthusiasm and orderly organisation. Fai Henry Fonye examines the significance of the event and takes the opportunity to review our dream of a new and great Cameroon. He says our old hopes of reunification and bilingualism are being reached, while new horizons of real democracy and social justice beckon us:*

The historic nation-wide celebrations marking the 14th anniversary of the peaceful revolution of May 20, characterized by lengthy march pasts and cultural activities have come and gone for the year.

In the nation's capital, the Cameroon Head of State, His Excellency Paul Biya personally presided over a three-hour-long march past, part of which was an unprecedented military parade during which units of the air force and the army displayed Cameroon's might of the barrel. Of course, the police band that orchestrated the march past was most colourful and at its best.

A number of points are significant about this year's May 20 celebrations. First, the organisation was better as it left traditional dances in their provinces, enabled the entire nation to feel the pulse and vibrations of the national feast and solved the problem of accommodation at the nation's capital.

Second, the numerous messages of congratulations from other countries demonstrated that Cameroon has many friends in the world and can count on their generosity, charity, goodwill and cooperation.

Last but not least, the representatives of the French government that is, the French Communication and Culture Minister, François Leotard and Special Adviser on African Affairs to the President, French Guy Penn could not help observing that the enthusiastic participation in the ceremonies by the youth and women was concrete proof of the popularity of President Paul Biya.

There is no doubt that as an individual, President Paul Biya could be popular, especially when one looks at his policies and social action. But since good leadership cannot be a one man show, we should like this popularity to be true of the collective leadership of our country.

There are still people who for selfish reasons continue to cast doubts on the credibility of our government either by their direct executive and confused action or by their toxic advice. Some of them are fired but still return in full force to positions of authority and influence as if they were indispensable or as if there were no other competent Cameroonians at hand. This confuses the masses who are entitled to information unless that kind of information was likely to jeopardize the security of the state.

If liberty and equality are chiefly to be found in democracy, they will be best attained when all persons alike share in the government to the utmost.

Since the New Deal, we prided ourselves with a government which derives its power from the consent of the governed that is from the people through their representatives which in this case, is our entire National Assembly. From those same people must come the dreams, the faith, the hopes and the works which fashion the great purpose of our government. We must never let this ideal character of this country to perish. We are making progress, but we must aim at higher and higher standards of democracy and human rights.

Nevertheless, we still hold fast on to our dream of a new and great Cameroon. We have the opportunity to move not only toward the prosperous and powerful society, but upward toward a really just and great society in Africa. Our old hopes of reunification and bilingualism are being reached while new horizons of real democracy and especially social justice beckon us. Indeed our country remains the land of the great experiment in Africa.

Cameroon can be a place where each child can grow up knowing that success in life depends only on his ability and not on tribe, club, clique or the creed of his religion. It can be a place where we are growing not only richer and stronger, but happier and wiser. For whatever the strength of our arms, or whatever the size of our economy, we will not be that new and great nation unless we pursue excellence.

The new society of our dreams should be a challenge constantly renewed, driving us toward a destiny where the meaning of our lives matches the products of our labour. And here, there are three central places where we must begin to build that great nation: in our towns, in our rural areas, and especially in our classrooms.

Aristotle said "men come together in cities in order to live, but they remain together in order to live the good life". It is harder and harder to live the good life in our growing cities and towns today. The catalogue of ills is long. Apart from the harassment from thieves and armed robbers, there is the decay of the centres and the despoiling of the outskirts.

Many people live in squalor because there is not enough housing for our people while the landlords continue to exploit the situation in spite of government pronouncements and promises to check and penalize them. Worst of all, expansion of our young cities and towns without adequate planning is eroding the precious and time-honoured values of community with neighbours and communion with nature. We must execute our town plans, if there have been any, because the loss of these values breeds loneliness and boredom and indifference.

A second place where we must begin to build that new and great Cameroon is in our rural areas. This point has been stressed time without count, but so much lip service continues to be paid to it while rural exodus continues an upward trend. To take our own example, how many well trained journalists live in our countryside to report on the activities of the people? The best journalists live in cities or towns and report mostly about the activities of big people and city or town events so that the urban-rural gap widens and national integration becomes an illusion.

A third place to build a new and great Cameroon is in our classrooms. Here we are talking seriously about education. For it is in our classrooms that our children's lives will be shaped. Our country cannot become great until every young mind is set free to scan the farthest reaches of thought and imagination. Here, the social action of our Head of State, His Excellency Paul Biya has been remarkable. But for so many other reasons, we are still far from that goal.

Today, several thousands have dropped out of primary and high schools. Each year, thousands of high school graduates with proven ability do not enter university because of limited opportunity. We certainly need more universities and other educational institutions to match our fast growing population.

In many places, classrooms are overcrowded and curricula are outdated. Most of our qualified teachers are underpaid and many of our well paid teachers are unqualified. We must give every child a place to sit and a teacher to learn from.

Poverty must not be a bar to learning, and learning must offer an escape from poverty. But more classrooms and more teachers are not enough. We must seek an educational system which grows in quality as well as in size. This means better training for our teachers. It means exploring new techniques of teaching, to find new ways to stimulate the love for learning and the capacity for creation. The mass media, especially with the coming of television, should supplement or complement that effort.

But as far as this commentator knows, there is no organized educational broadcasting in Cameroon like what happens with success in countries like the Ivory Coast, Nigeria and Tanzania. Memoranda have been submitted to our authorities in this direction but they have never had the courtesy to give an official reply, be it negative.

Nevertheless, these are three of the central issues of a new and potentially great society: the city or town, the countryside and the classroom.

While our government has many programmes directed at these issues, we cannot pretend that we have the full answers to those problems. This is the time we should assemble the best thoughts in our country and the broadest knowledge from all over the world to find the answers for our potentially great country, Cameroon.

Fai Henry Fonye

Cameroon Report 01/6/1986: The CPDM and Civil Liberties

Introduction: *The forces of law and order have recently been engaging is senseless and brutal disregard of the rights of the individual and these acts of violence have led to the death of several citizens who in all the cases had committed no crimes that warranted their fate. The recent shooting of Emmanuel Kwende, a shopkeeper in Yaounde for allegedly violating traffic regulation and the shooting in Nso of an army officer who was merely intervening to prevent a gendarme colleague from shooting a citizen have brought to focus the increasingly disturbing issue of indiscipline in the forces of law and order. Fai Henry Fonye has come up with some pertinent observations about violence practiced by forces of law and order:*

The democratic elections of the basic organs of the national party and the enthusiasm of the just ended seminars confirm our strong belief in the important role of the Cameroon Peoples Democratic Movement CPDM in nation building.

One of the new hopes of the CPDM was to propose to Cameroonians a new way of living together, a new understanding of their rights and obligation, a new nation of political militancy and a bolder step towards national integration, the guarantee of peace, stability and prosperity.

On the 20th of March 1985 in Bamenda, the national President of the party, Paul Biya explained the new motto – Unity – Progress – Democracy as endowed with a new dynamism and mobilization. Above all that new motto underscored among other things, the administration of justice and ensuring the security of the citizen, his property and his rights. Such ambition means that the party should count on enlightened and frank militants who are critical and open with respect for civic discipline, thus expressing the desire for constructive democracy and the seriousness of a responsible people.

It is in that spirit of enlightened, frank criticism that Cameroon Report comes out to condemn acts that have of recent tended to undermine the security of the citizen and civic discipline in our society.

Just a few days ago, a young man was shot dead here in Yaounde. Barely a month ago, an army officer was shot in Nso. He later died in a hospital in Yaounde. Sometime ago another youth was carelessly killed in Buea.

These shootings, as sporadic and isolated as they may appear bring surges of emotions and tears, particularly to the immediate relatives and like ice-bergs, these incidents point to hidden but dangerous signs for the people. But we must realize that people usually face big problems because they have neglected to solve small ones.

The militants of the CPDM must be more vigilant in order to detect and fight against anything that could hinder the continuity of our options of peace and any possible threat to the security of citizens. The CPDM as a veritable framework for civic and political education must point out these evils that tend to disunite the people to the appropriate quarters.

The government and the CPDM should ensure that sound legislative policies are made to protect citizens against the aggressions of others seeking to push their freedoms or their power too far. Officers in positions of authority and discipline must bear down hard to make their men behave and deal in a friendly respectful way with the masses. Incidents of barbaric behaviour anywhere in the country can only bring discredit to the forces of law and order and the nation.

There is perhaps no task more complex, except possibly the task of government itself, than that of engendering in a democracy an appreciation of the role of members of the forces of law and order who especially decide to be careless. Crude, carousing officers playing tough in bars, night clubs and elsewhere can do much to offset the image of a respectable profession. The forces of law and order must themselves obey the law, while enforcing the law. This way, they will demonstrate their moral fervour for the dignity of man.

Those responsible for the shootings may be tried and even sentenced in accordance with the laws of the Republic, even with the objectivity and dignity characteristic of a good judicial system. But who wants to lose his or her relative, just because there is a possibility of eventually punishing the criminal? Human life is sacred and cannot be exchanged for anything else.

And it must be pointed out here in time that those who happen to be victims of these shootings tend to come from one part of the Republic and that is dangerous to peace and national unity – let alone national integration. Cameroonians generally have great respect for human life and are attached to human values and the virtues from which they have always drawn their strength, grandeur and pride. We cannot afford to throw away these identities.

From a much more general perspective, the behaviour of these officers can destroy the confidence that citizens have in the administration of their country. As the Cameroon Head of State, His Excellency Paul Biya once observed, it should be understood that citizen's approval or disapproval of policy being carried out by government with the support of the party is sometimes dependent on the type of relations that exist between the citizen and government services.

This means that the performances of services may influence in a decisive way the attitudes of our fellow citizens towards our principles and ideals. They may win the enthusiasm of citizens or give rise to disillusion, discontent and demobilization. That is why the discipline of the members of the forces of law and order should never be in doubt.

Fai Henry Fonye

38

News talk 24/6/86: Enemies of Democracy*

Introduction: *On Sunday June 22nd Cameroon Report failed to come on the air as it is customary on Sunday mornings. The non-broadcast of the programme was the result of a ban for which no one is yet prepared to accept official responsibility, a ban which did not take the usual administrative form as is expected in matters of such importance. Analysts and commentators of the programme arrived the station last Friday to find a casually scribbled note on the notice board informing them that Cameroon Report had been suspended and that it should be replaced by a watered – down version to be called News Panorama, a newsreel format that should eschew opinion, criticism and commentary. This outrageous decision, fraught with administrative irregularities and backed by a faceless authority, was taken without prior consultation with the editors. The handwritten banning note offered no reasons for the suspension. The editors viewed the move as an anti-democratic act and resolved to begin a series of new talks on the New Deal Government. In the first of the series tonight, Sam-Nuvala Fonkem talks on the enemies of democracy:*

Talking about the enemies of democracy, I would like to go back to last Sunday, 22nd June, when Cameroonians were deprived of their favourite programme, Cameroon Report. Last Sunday, our commentator read this epitaph to mark the death of Cameroon Report and which I am going to quote: "Here lies a programme in peace, not in pieces; it served the wind of change selflessly, yet it died. But it learned something; the forces against democracy are apparently stronger than the forces for democracy. The forces against change are more committed than the forces for change, and the buffoonery keeps over-flowing."

For tonight's news talk, I would like to insist on just three points: That "yet it died" secondly, "the forces against democracy", and thirdly, "the buffoonery keeps overflowing". I wish to say before we go into the depth of our commentary or news talk, since we have been banned from making commentaries but our news talk tonight will dwell on democracy and the New Deal Government.

It has been very clear all along that when Mr Paul Biya's Government came in Cameroon with the promise of New Deal democracy, freedom of expression, constructive criticism, we are witnesses to the fact that some people are against constructive democracy, of constructive criticism which means that some people are not necessarily against New Deal, but they feel that somehow they can make a deal without a new one.

Contrary to our commentator, last Sunday, 22nd June, 1986, Cameroon Report did actually die. What happened was this: a couple of bunch of idiots thought they could take a decision to stop a programme which falls within a New Deal Government in Cameroon. Because why, I will explain to you. They knew that Mr Paul Biya's Government, amongst all the achievements, the most outstanding has been constructive criticism, and I Sam- Nuvala Fonkem, since we hate referring to ourselves as this reporter, I, Sam- Nuvala Fonkem, believes very strongly that the greatest achievement of Mr Paul Biya's Government has been the fact of constructive criticism and that anybody who is against constructive criticism is certainly against Mr Paul Biya's New Deal Government.

Secondly, we are talking about monkeys who want to discredit Mr Paul Biya's Government. Whoever went to parliament to discredit a programme acknowledged, cherished, by the Cameroonian population, to stop that kind of a programme in parliament, should first of all, have the mandate of the people to stop that kind of a programme that deals with the people of Cameroon. That a parliamentarian who fails to win election in his village, in his constituency, should sit up in a committee meeting in parliament, without the unanimity of parliament, decide what is good for the people, we in Cameroon Report, and every right thinking Cameroonian should know that such an action is subversive.

That a member of parliament who has no legitimacy of representation of his people, who has been sacked in a free and fair election* *, brought about by the New Deal Government, instead of sitting in parliament as a hand-clapper, should be given the opportunity to sit up in parliament, make proposals, that should deprive the Cameroon population of what the Cameroonian people deem fit for our society, today in 1986, less than 20 years to the year 2000...

We beg to differ in this programme and in this profession and in Radio Cameroon... that we shall listen to the populace, but not through the voice of an individual who represents nobody in Cameroon to begin with, who has been voted out of political representation, who shall sit in parliament to make a suggestion that shall affect the executive arm of government and that such decisions shall be taken to the deprivation of Cameroonians... we in Cameroon Report want to say that when last Sunday our reporter said it died, it did not die, not because of a selfish individual, parochial, sectionalist, tribalistic, unrepresentative, represents nothing... we have to take leave to differ.

We hope that such decisions that are made in parliament, the representatives of the people of Cameroon, in an era of the New Deal, where the New Deal opens out clearly, that there shall be constructive criticism, and there shall be democratic representation of the people. That for an individual to take upon himself to influence executive decision, we of this profession, God bless us, we differ from it and hope that the New Deal shall be created with everybody involved, not just politicians, particularly politicians who cannot even win elections. But thank God, we shall do our job in the Radio, and that democracy has come to stay and will stay in Cameroon.

Footnote:

* This commentary which sparked off controversy and led to a 4-month detention of the commentator and two other colleagues EBSSY NGUM (who had written and read the epitaph that announced the death of CR the previous Sunday) and Johnnie MacViban (who read the evening news in which the news talk was presented) was delivered extemporaneously and heatedly, hence the uncharacteristic jumpiness of the syntax and diction. The charge of contempt of authority (outrage a corps constitué) was proffered against the commentator after the investigating magistrate discovered a charge of defamation could not be made to stick because there was no plaintiff. A case of contempt of authority involving a journalist of the official media was unprecedented. It ended with a face-saving verdict of a one year suspended sentence over a 3-year period.

** Refers to election to the local executive of the ruling party, as opposed to parliamentary election.

Sam- Nuvala Fonkem

African & World Affairs

39

Cameroon Report 22/7/1980: Towards a New World Information Order

Introduction: *More than 100 delegates of information from all over Africa have gathered in Yaounde for the first ever UNESCO-sponsored conference on information. The conference, dubbed "Africa 80" is being chaired by UNESCO director-general Mahtar Mbow of Senegal. The delegates including Information Ministers, Directors of state-owned media establishments, communication experts of international organisations and journalists would discuss the setting up of a new world information order to redress the imbalance of information flow between the industrialised nations and the Third World.*

Among several topics to be discussed are the heavy dependency of the Third World on Western communication facilities, the one-sided flow of information from the West to the Third World, the distorted image of the Third World as presented by the western media and the encouragement of rural-based media in African countries. The conference will seek to elicit commitments from African countries to increase investments in the communication sector. As delegates settle down to deliberate on what is expected to result in an African communication policy, Sam-Nuvala Fonkem cautions in the following commentary against the temptation by African governments to adopt an authoritarian position on communication media:

At a time when most African states have attained post independence maturity, the need to define and apply an appropriate communication strategy has become more pertinent than ever before. As the decolonisation process is getting nearer to its end, Africa is increasingly faced with the problem of neo-colonialism which is most evident in its communication system, a communication system which is strongly linked to the colonial metropolis.

It has become more imperative than ever before to decolonise communication in Africa. This means that, as President Ahidjo clearly warned in his inaugural address today, "African states are running the great risk of having their freedom of judgement trampled upon and their personality disintegrated, if the presentation of biased, depressing and often catastrophic news continued". Africa never comes into the limelight of news unless there is a coup d'état or something as sensational and catastrophic as that.

It has been widely accepted or agreed upon that the present flow of information is one sided and that Africa is seen through the eyes of foreigners and that for a true image of Africa to be presented, the information should emanate from within not without. Nevertheless, this commentator would like to warn that the rectification of this situation should not mean the replacement of an external information tyranny with one that would want to see things its own way and not consider the other side of the coin.

Formulating a strategy to decolonise the African communication system is not enough. African states must be prepared to sacrifice for an autonomous communication system and be prepared to funnel some of the fat sums of money lavished on meaningless pomp and pageantry to support such a system. To get quality means money and any African government today which wants an efficient communication system must pay for it or stop dreaming about a decolonised system.

This commentator would also like to warn that the Yaounde conference on communication policies in Africa should not be used as a forum to adopt measures that would stifle the growth of a free press, otherwise the whole purpose of decolonising information for a fairer and more truthful presentation of the African image would be destroyed. Some countries are already applying measures that would eventually limit the growth of a free press and we hope the conference would deplore such measures.

When a liberal profession like journalism is placed under the total control of the executive arm of government, then we must admit that it is the beginning of authoritarianism which we hope the conference would denounce. We can't have authoritarianism and expect to have a free press and we hope the conference would deplore such measures. And any press that is not free can truly reflect the thinking and diverse views of its readership or audience. You can't eat your cake and have it.

Sam-Nuvala Fonkem

Cameroon Report 12/04/1981: Africa's Five Million Refugees

Introduction: *Delegates from more than one hundred countries met in Geneva this week to discuss the issue of aid to African Refugees. In examining the plight of more than five million refugees in Africa, George Ngwa points out that perhaps the real answer to the African refugee problem is for international charitable organisations to strive more to get to the root cause of the problem such as drought and political instability.*

Up from three million in 1979, African refugees today number five million, which is at best a conservative estimate. They are victims of Africa's gruesome diary of recurrent natural and man-made disasters such as drought and poor harvests, compounded by sheer neglect, mismanagement and convoluted political policies which, of late, have formed an explosive combination and sent hundreds of thousands of refugees scurrying for safety, but ironically running into almost certain death.

Though half of the world so far has shown only bemused interest in African refugees, like their kin from Haiti, they received scant attention from the world press. World attention has instead gravitated towards the "boat" and "foot" people of South East Asia, making their plight more dramatic than the potentially deadly situation in Africa.

With due sympathy to the plight of the "boat" and "foot" people, there were, no doubt, political considerations behind the so many United Nations convened conferences to pledge millions of dollars for South East Asian refugees.

Fortunately, African refugees have benefitted from the continent's legendary hospitality. Whenever they have shown up they have been welcomed and treated not as refugees but as displaced brothers and human beings. Though some unscrupulous civil servants with the tacit approval of their governments have fed fat on relief supplies, the refugees, on the whole, have been encouraged to be self-sufficient, grow as much of their own food as they can and build improved accommodation and facilities for themselves.

One of the greatest problems has arisen from nomadic refugees who often take advantage of Africa's fluid borders to become wandering destitute instead of staying in refugee camps. This has made the provision of emergency relief supplies extremely difficult for the continent which could comfortably solve its refugee problem if this generous act of sharing with a distressed brother were not putting a strain on many rural communities who barely have enough for themselves.

In this light, the just-ended United National-sponsored international conference on aid to refugees in Africa – ICARA is commendable though it should have been held years ago. With some six hundred million dollars marshalled from the nearly one hundred countries which attended, the conference has demonstrated that the international community is capable of speedy action to alleviate human suffering.

The conference has also shown that the refugee problem in Africa cannot be solved by relief action alone. There must be follow-up programmes aimed at integrating refugees into new communities. The big question is whether this is feasible. Tanzania has demonstrated that the problem can be solved if countries, away from the big refugee areas, offer refugees a home.

Perhaps the real answer to the African refugee problem is for international charitable organisations to strive more to get to the root cause and identify situations which might give rise to people fleeing their homes. The United Nations High Commission for Refugees certainly does a good job helping victims of conflicts, but more thought ought to be given as to how the flow of refugees can be stemmed.

Of all human tragedies, to be daily uncertain about the future, to wonder what will happen to your children, to be totally dependent on the charity of others is worse than degrading.

George Ngwa

Cameroon Report 07/7/1981: Boycotting sporting links with Racist South African

Introduction: *The racist Springboks rugby team of South Africa is in New Zealand for a tour in defiance of international condemnation. Akwanka Joe Ndifor condemns the Springboks' tour and the double standards of Western nations who pretend to condemn racism yet condone sporting relations with South Africa's apartheid regime:*

In the eyes of whites in general and the criminals of the Pretoria regime in racist South Africa in particular, whoever has a black skin is a fool and must remain a fool. And that is why the western nations should deceive themselves by feeling that they can convince Africans to separate sports from politics when it comes to protecting western selfish interests.

It is about time we determine who the real fool is. Time and time again, we have condemned racial segregation in general and racist South Africa in particular. We have persistently called for a boycott of sporting links with the criminal regime in Pretoria.

In spite of the fact that the liars in Washington, London and in Paris before the accession to power of the Mitterrand government, have pretended to condemn racial discrimination in South Africa, they have continued to use their internal veto at the United Nations to block punitive measures against the criminal Pretoria regime.

Once again, there is a general feeling among Western circles that sports must be separated from politics. And that is why they have failed to condemn South Africa's racist Springboks rugby tour of New Zealand.

We now understand why the westerners gave a deaf ear to African pleas for a boycott of the Montreal Olympics in 1976 because of sporting ties between the Pretoria gang and this very notorious New Zealand which was to attend the games.

The Carter regime in Washington made it clear it would not boycott the games because, as Jimmy Carter put it, sports must not meddle with politics. Foolishly enough, after the Soviet invasion of Afghanistan in December 1979, Mr Carter was the first to call on African states to boycott the 1980 Moscow Olympics. And he felt he could fool Africans by sending a mere boxer who is ignorant about politics to come and convince African leaders about the issue. Asked by an American reporter whether he was not contradicting himself, Mr Carter said sports must be separated from politics but not war. We begin to question whether war is not politics or a consequence of politics.

Maybe Washington forgets that the next Olympic Games will take place in Los Angeles in the United States. Those African countries which happened to have mistakenly taken sides with Washington in boycotting the Moscow Olympics must understand that a complete African boycott of the games must be put into effect if New Zealand is allowed to participate.

If that country will defy world opinion and condone with racists, then we are not prepared to take sides with it. The Commonwealth ministerial conference which was supposed to take place in that country will no longer take place there as a measure of protest. Harsher measures are even necessary. And the real fools must understand that in fact, Africans are not monkeys as they claim.

Africans are now fed up with the veto they face every year in trying to impose mandatory sanctions against the Pretoria clique at the United Nations. Other alternatives should be sought.

If Morocco can make the OAU catch a cold with its threat of withdrawal, then we don't understand why African nations cannot make a massive walk out of the United Nations to show the gravity of the issue of liberation of the oppressed people of Azania.

Akwanka Joe Ndifor

Cameroon Report 23/08/1981: The Proposed Senegambian confederation

Introduction: *We in Cameroon Report don't want to be seen as contradicting our avowed commitment to African solidarity. Just that you must stand on your feet and on solid ground before trying to rescue someone who is sinking in mud. After self-sufficiency is attained, it is possible that two neighbouring countries contribute so much to each other's well-being that they fancy becoming one. Such is the kind of marriage that Senegal and Gambia are talking about. As sovereign nations, they have the right – no less than Chad and Libya- to discuss marriage as long as it is the decision of the people of both countries. Cameroonians, as people living that kind of marriage, can only hope for the would-be Senegambia republic that each of the partners is laying out all the cards on the table and keeping none in the sleeve. But then, what are the odds against the proposed marriage? Epah Fonkeng has these observations:*

For the second time since he became Gambian Chief of State, Sir Dawda Jawara is said to have proposed a confederation between his country and Senegal with which it already has a mutual defence pact. Such association may sound like a welcome commitment to Nkrumah's Pan Africanist vision, more so in the contemporary geopolitical set up in which the small and the weak must close up ranks or stand to be crushed one after the other. Notwithstanding, certain observations are bound to be advanced.

What does a state with all the equations in its disfavour go to seek in a wedlock with another that is eight times its size, with a population ratio of five to one and has a more telling position, economically? Is it the due and legitimate need for African unity? Or maybe the raison d'être is found in the ethnic, religious and cultural homogeneity of both states that proponents are wont to invoke?

These observations which require clarity would seem to indicate a contending stand against the venture in motion, even though it is not the case. Realpolitik however, warrants guarded optimism and caution. To place all of one's trump cards on the table and hope for an easy win is a false contention that man does, or can live, by bread alone, to borrow a biblical dictum. The belaboured theme of unity which could gradually and with ease pass for a deadening torpor seems to seek vindication in an equally defective notion of cultural parallelism.

Ethnically, both countries are overwhelmingly Wolof. In this connection, the parallel could be drawn from what political sociologists have termed the public and private realms in which they assert that in the so-called new states of Africa, the commitment to and reverence for the private or more individualistic and localised realm – for example the ethnic group – by far supersedes that which is of the public realm, in this case, that which is of the state.

Consequently, the analyst in his crave for easy solutions may be tempted to utter a sigh of relief at the thought that the people of both states are likely to give more substance to their belonging to a common ethnic group or private realm than to their public realms, which are their respective colonial heritages, particularly as far as a superimposed foreign language is concerned. Yet, according to our analysis, the English and French-oriented background in the wider Senegambian context now incidentally takes the place of the private realm, and hence commands much more adherence and sympathy.

Even without inverting the order of our consideration, the outcome is still likely to be a firmer identification within each sub-cultural or linguistic group. This could result in a possible schism in the new public realm i.e. a bilingual Senegambia that becomes the new dominant – submissive framework, a conceptual framework that has proved particularly relevant in analysing the competitive allocation of scare resources in pluralist societies.

The two sub-cultures would then be characterised, the one by an imposing foreign language, the other by a submissive foreign language, and the allocation of resources would then be invariably conditioned by the nature of relationships with the dominant sub-culture which would incidentally have the upper hand and would be drawing advantages from a now visibly more powerful economic, geographical and numerical position.

It would then not be correct to assert in that instance that African unity-nay, African nationalism, triumphed over European imperialism, and right to postulate that in the encounter between two African sub-nationalisms, (so to speak, because the weapons in use are not originally African), one sub-nationalism did carry hands up to the other.

Francis Epah Fonkeng

43

Cameroon Report 04/10/1981: The I.M.F. Tightens policy towards Third World

Introduction: *The annual meeting of the International Monetary Fund I.M.F. and the World Bank has ended in Washington with rich nations committed to further belt-tightening and poor nations left with little hope of increased aid. In his closing remarks to a nearly empty convention hall, I.M.F. Managing Director Jacques De La Rosière said the four-day meeting had produced a clear consensus on what he called a widespread and compelling need for strong policies of economic adjustment in member countries. Poor nations had come to the meeting to seek a substantial increase in aid to offset global problems of chronic inflations, high interest rates and unemployment. But American President Ronald Reagan set a gloomy tone of egoism when he told delegates that his plan to revive the American economy left no room for the United States, the biggest source of funds for the I.M.F. and the World Bank, to increase aid to the two organisations. George NGWA examines the implications of Mr Reagan's statement:*

The American demand for tougher conditions on loans from the I.M.F. to countries with balance of payment problems was, to say the least, a slap in the face of poor nations.

Granted that it has been widely accepted for some time now that the advent of the new masters in the White House marks a fundamental change of policy, the manner in which they have been singing the praises of an economic free-for-all has proved a surprise nonetheless. President Reagan and his team must be credited with the guts of presenting themselves to the poor nations, to borrow the words of one delegate, as ugly Americans.

For one thing, not only did the Reagan administration, backed by Britain, West Germany and Japan (with more reluctant support from France) prove insensitive to calls for more assistance from developing countries, they even talked of reorganising the World Bank, intimating in the process that this would amount to far more stringent conditions for cheap credits and outright grants as well as the freezing of special drawing rights for the poorest countries.

In this gloomy atmosphere, calls from the third world for an annual increase of at least 13.8 billion dollars in funding for the I.M.F. fell at the wayside while supply-side economics was the order of the day to the detriment of the economies of poor countries.

The austere tone adopted by Mr Reagan is certain to block the chances of any break-through at the next rich and poor nations' confrontation later this month in Cancun - Mexico. That would be unfortunate, for the malaise gripping the economies of most nations would remain a fixture for some time with repercussions on the economies of those countries which claim to be safe.

Further intensification of poverty causes social, economic and political disorder in developing countries with severe repercussions on world peace. That's inter-dependence.

History would judge 1981 as a watershed in North-South relations. It would be a year in which all nations moved forward in a concerted attack on economic disparities or alternatively one in which they allowed a momentous opportunity to slip through their fingers. Major changes should be made to create an international system sensitive to the needs of all.

In other words, the world monetary institutions should be restructured to cope with the reality of Third World poverty. We are in a fog and in this fog the American co-pilot must change course, otherwise all of us will perish.

George Ngwa

Cameroon Report 11/10/1981: The Assassination of SADAT: Consequences on Egyptian Politics

Introduction: *Egyptian leader Mohammed Anwar El Sadat is no more. He was assassinated last Tuesday by gunmen as he sat watching the closing stages of the annual October 6th military parade. Mr Sadat sat in the grand stand, flanked by members of government senior officials and diplomats. As jets roared overhead in acrobatic stunts and trucks rumbled below, four soldiers jumped out of their lorry and began running towards the reviewing stand. President Sadat, believing the soldiers were coming forward to salute him, stood up to acknowledge their greeting. But instead, they opened fire with automatic AK 47 rifles and grenades. One of the presidential body guards leapt on the 62 year-old Egyptian leader to provide him cover while shooting dead one of the assailants. The commotion lasted thirty seconds and by the time it was over, President Sadat was hit five times in the chest and neck. As the astonished crowd dived for safety, Mr Sadat, already in a coma and coughing blood, was rushed off to the Mahdi military hospital south of the capital, Cairo where he underwent two hours of open heart surgery to no avail. He was officially pronounced dead several hours later. Mr Sadat was a towering figure in the Middle East and the world stage. Neither his admirers not his critics would deny that his death would have a profound impact on the Middle East region. Three most important events in the region can be ascribed to Mr Sadat, namely the 1973 Arab-Israeli war in which Egypt emerged victorious. Mr Sadat's dramatic visit to Jerusalem in 1977 and the signing of an Egyptian-Israeli peace treaty known as the Camp David Accords in 1979. Sa*m- *Nuvala Fonkem, our Middle East* *watcher, attempts to see if these momentous changes in the Middle East and the situations they created can survive the death of their principal architect:*

The assassination of President Sadat has left many political observers pondering over a number of perplexing questions such as the safeguard of political and ideological continuity in Egypt and the future of Middle East peace negotiations.

Ever since the late President made his historic visit to Jerusalem in 1977, the course of events in Egypt took a radical turn which caused no small anxiety to Muslim fundamentalists and politicians who felt bitter at what they saw as an unpardonable deviation from the stand against Zionism.

Mr. Sadat's new policy after extending his hand of friendship to Israel the arch-enemy of the Arab world included a movement from a centralised socialism inherited from his predecessor Nasser to a laissez-faire liberal type economy heavily inclined to the West. His break in relations with the Soviet Union and excessive friendly gestures towards the United States were enough to set the scene for violent opposition from the conservative camp.

In a recent bid to consolidate and foster his pro-western policies, Mr Sadat went out of his way to declare a systematic crackdown on his opponents, banning some political parties and ordering a mass arrest of members of the intelligentsia and religious fundamentalists who were critical of his policies.

The mistake he made was to confound active opposition with constructive criticism. It was Mr Sadat's inability to contain criticism which this reporter believes, was largely responsible for his hyper-sensitive reaction that provoked his ultimate assassination. So far, there are no indications that what happened in Egypt was an attempt to take over power, thus the assassination of Mr. Sadat was primarily aimed at eliminating an Arab leader whose personality had become a symbol of Arab disunity among Arab nations and a symbol of peace and vision to the rest of the world.

Although Mr Sadat's successor, President-designate Hosni Mubarak has pledged to continue Mr. Sadat's policies including the maintenance of peace with Israel, one must admit however that the absence of Mr. Sadat would affect the future course of those policies.

Mr. Mubarak would have to deal with growing political activism and opposition in Egypt and despite a pledge by the armed forces to remain loyal to Mr Sadat's policy, it would be a grievous mistake for Mr. Mubarak to pursue the violent suppression of anti-government critics. Mr Mubarak is faced with the tough decision on what to do with hundreds of political detainees arrested in the recent crackdown. It would be in his interest to release them as a first step towards re-establishing stability in the economy.

Mr. Mubarak would have to adopt a more conciliatory and compromising attitude towards the Muslim religious conservatives who, for several years, have watched with bitter consternation the continued Israeli military aggression in Lebanon.

The ever-increasing opposition to the Egyptian-Israeli peace treaty, long regarded by conservative Muslims as a sell-out will determine the course of events in Egypt. This would entail necessary modifications in Egypt's foreign policy and it is inevitable that such modifications would affect negotiations on Palestinian autonomy and the complete withdrawal of Israel from the Sinai. Any radical change in the political atmosphere in Egypt could increase the possibility of greater Soviet influence in the Middle East and the gradual erosion of America's reliance on Egypt as a close ally.

In effect, Egypt without Sadat can hardly remain the same again. Mr Sadat's personal victory in establishing peace with Israel was not shared by the entire Egyptian masses, thus his absence is bound to affect the continuity of his policies.

Although one may not foresee any drastic changes in Egyptian policies in the near future, the assassination of Mr Sadat and the impending threat of religious fanaticism and political activism have already created an atmosphere that could favour some kind of rapprochement between Egypt and its Arab critics.

Sam- Nuvala Fonkem

45

Cameroon Report 26/10/1981: The North-South Dialogue

Introduction: *The 22-nation summit on ending poverty in developing countries has ended in Cancun, Mexico without reaching full agreement on how to restart global negotiations on bridging the gap dividing the world's rich and poor nations. A statement by co-chairman Pierre Trudeau, the Canadian Prime Minister made clear that progress on a second major issue- the establishment of an energy affiliate of the World Bank to finance energy production in poor countries – was blocked by American opposition to the creation of new world financial institutions. As was expected, the United States was the only one of the 22 participants which included leaders of developing nations, which did not support multi-lateral aid schemes to the Third World. It was absolutely clear even before the conference in Cancun that some leaders of the Western capitalist World who went there had no intention of sacrificing their egoistic interests. Nevertheless, it was shocking that western leaders had agreed to a dialogue only because they believed it would allow the developing countries to let off steam about the current world economic order and thus postpone demands for change. Victor Epie Ngome sees the Cancun summit as a farce and an exercise in hypocrisy as demonstrated by the United States:*

For those who have not been to church for a long time, Cancun would have been a good place to go. What happened there strikes me as a two-day church service whose liturgy had been streamlined by prior tempering of the pent-up acerbities that would have revolted the powers that be.

Everybody seemed to have been pleasantly surprised at the untraditional non-polarity of the talks – but that's everybody who did not understand beforehand what the Third World leaders in Cancun understood – namely that with only 22 countries represented and about 130 seats vacant, no decisions could be made in Cancun – that the most one could reasonably expect from there, contrary to Lopez Portillo's plea, was agreement to negotiate. Another thing they understood was that even if Cancun had the power to make decisions, such decisions could only be carried if they pleased the power-wielding North and that the transfer of wealth that the South are asking for, is not of a nature to please.

Among those who were pleasantly surprised, or feigned to be, at the smoothness of the service, was the chief preacher from Washington. He had expected a lot of invectives from various quarters because in the eyes of most people, especially the third worlders, he has gained notoriety for preaching his own gospel and dogmatising without positive mission.

For one thing, his sermon in Cancun could afford to carry necessary militants to avoid unwarranted embarrassment and hostility, given that it was preceded by an epistle in Philadelphia in which he had spelt out the dogma as bluntly as only he could – with a resultant awareness of the Cancun congregation of the futility of any attempt to put up a fight.

His speaking with a rare dose of suavity thus made Cancun business easy –namely everybody else listening in all docility to lessons on how to run their economies.

Only, at a certain point in the sermon you thought you were listening to self-indulgent prayer of the Pharisee: I have done more for the poor than all those publicans; I have given them more alms. I have bought more of their goods. In short what I have done for them is enormous and still plan to do more on condition that they take my advice, and my advice is this: that when they talk to me they should be practical and specific, focussing on what can be done and on obstacles that can be removed.

- 2. That they should respect the competence and powers of those banks in which my influence is paramount.

- 3. That whatever they asked me to do for them must benefit me in some way (I may be good but I am not God).

- 4. That they will desist from confronting me – (I may be wrong or right, wise or unwise, fair unfair – that is not relevant. It is fact).

The congregation of alms-beggars listened to this sermon in reverent silence, conscious that if they dared raise a voice they could be taken off the alms mailing list.

But while the preacher pats himself on the back and blows his own trumpet (which nobody seems to have breath and conviction to blow for him), the emotional stress of Southern members of the congregation is seeking ways take it out on someone. They choose the most conspicuous absentee – who is neither a Christian nor a Muslim. Generally, the absentee is always wrong, but this particular absentee was the publican who did not even dare to approach the walls of the synagogue because, according to the Pharisee, he had nothing to offer the alms seekers.

And while everybody spills their venom and condemns Moscow in abstentia, all the absentee cares to say is that the poor need alms because the Pharisee extorted them of their wealth to begin with. The Southerners know this, but perhaps this was the wrong time to remind them, when they have been told that fairness doesn't matter – that what matters is fact – and that fact is that wealth now belongs somewhere and that's from where the terms for sharing it must emanate.

And so the service ended and the faithful poor are returning home full, not of the Holy Spirit but of the futility of any attempt to win sympathy for their plight. They have agreed that global negotiations are needed, and urgently, but they have been told by the preacher's consultant what they must never forget: namely, seek ye first our kingdom and all things shall be added unto you.

Victor Epie Ngome

Cameroon Report 13/12/1981, Ciskei Homeland: Another stride for Apartheid

Introduction: *Independent Africa again stood helplessly by as racist South Africa made another stride in its experiment in herding 23 million blacks into barren patches of land and granting them so-called independence. When one realises what fate befell the American Red Indians and the Australian aborigines, South Africa's bantustanisation of its indigenous population can only mean one thing – the gradual elimination of blacks in Azania. Unfortunately this is going on with the complicity of some of those who claim to be leaders of their peoples. African leaders must stand up to the challenge the fascist Pretoria regime is making by granting fake independence to the Bantustans or so-called homeland. Our commentator, Victor Epie Ngome, says that the plight of the black man at the southern extreme of the continent – is a festering sore in the hearts of many thinking Africans – at least those who have not yet killed their consciences.*

I say this because there does exist a small group of Africans whose sensitivity to human suffering has been deadened by the leprosy of power, whether this be the suffering of distant brethren in Azania and Namibia, or of those within their immediate power- whose future they very conveniently trade off.

It is to this category of Africans that we speak today as we turn our spotlight on the fourth in their genre in South Africa. We don't talk to whites in South Africa for they are hard of hearing – even deaf when it is the voice of equity speaking. And it is naive to expect them to be otherwise, of their own accord, as if mistletoe would willingly quit a tree on which it is living healthily.

White South Africa must prosper as a nation – and prosperity today means maximum output from minimum input, and this minimum input is black man power which is ten times cheaper than white man-power. Prosperity also means the fruit of this maximum output being shared between as few people as possible and for South Africa, this means sharing the wealth, beginning with 86% of the arable land among the white minority after the black majority has been denationalised – because the creation of so-called independent homelands is tantamount to making the native blacks non South Africans and whose only asset will be the right to continue to export cheap labour, to permit the rich whites to maximise their profit. That is why we don't talk to the racist, because they can't hear us.

We don't even talk to Patrick Ephephu, Lucas Mangope or Kaiser Matanzima – who sold their brethren for power and wealth by accepting so-called independence on a silver platter for Venda, Bophutatswana and Transkei homelands respectively. We don't talk to them because they sold their ears first and do not even pretend to hear the voice of reason.

The one we talk to is the hat-donning moral replica of Idi Amin – who incidentally bears the same name as a notorious American horse thief. We talk to Lennox Sebe – the so-called chief of South Africa's fourth Bantustan for abusing the word independence. We talk to him because he is the first of the four to pretend to hear – to pretend that the acceptance of Pretoria's version of independence is the will of Ciskei people – because he preceded it with a phoney referendum in which only his own blind supporters voted without an honest exposure of the terms of the referendum whose result nobody could contest without being brutalised or detained – without trial.

We talk to him, neither because we think he really hears, nor because we doubt the eventual ability of the Ciskei people to scrap him and his treachery when they know the truth and get the chance, but because we fear that his spirit is wandering in Africa like Cain – and it is time Africans who have not been duped already, learned to scan beyond the cosmetics of principles like independence and referenda, before espousing them.

Ciskeians must be dumb to be satisfied for any length of time with an independence recognised only in one capital in the whole wide world – namely Pretoria, the capital of a regime that thrives on down treading the black man. What must they be thinking of non-recognition by the O.A.U? That Africans envy their independence? Or that there is no place for anymore flags in Addis Ababa? What must they be thinking of non-recognition even from white countries – even from those who have done the same thing and worse to the native inhabitants of the lands they now occupy? Do they think they will be able to survive the depopulation that the Red Indians were unable to survive in the hands of white American?

When we imagine that the first natives of the land of liberty, now living in what is tantamount to homelands, are today less than a fifth of their original population, when other populations are doubling; when we know that the aborigine women of Australia are being sterilized to reduce their population; when we know that some of these peoples have been subjected to genocide treatments like induced epidemics of measles and excessive protein diets; when we know that this has happened in some of the most avowedly puritan countries, and that the South African is the white man with the least pretension to any shade of concern for rectitude, it becomes evident that if the present trend of mock independence is not checked, the black in South Africa is an endangered species.

Victor Epie Ngome

Cameroon Report 17/01/1982: Palestinian Autonomy

Introduction: *There is still no break-through in the deadlock between Egypt and Israel over proposed Palestinian autonomy talks. After discussions with Egyptian leaders, U.S. Secretary of State Alexander Haig said he was encouraged by progress made so far, but a report carried by the authoritative Cairo daily newspaper Al Ahram said Egypt's position on the autonomy talks remains the same as at the beginning of the negotiations two years ago. The Israelis, who are pressing for an agreement by April 25 - for fear of losing their only leverage when they hand over the Sinai Peninsula to Egypt in three months time, say they will make no further concessions. Against this background, news analyst Ben Bongang wonders whether the American Secretary of state had any grounds for optimism:*

It would be naive at the moment to express any optimism for a dramatic solution to the problem of Palestinian autonomy which is, in effect, the real cause for all the upheavals the Middle East has experienced and lived with all these years.

If anything at all, Mr Haig's Middle East tour has the only merit of reminding some of the parties concerned and the international community of America's interest and determination to be the centre of all negotiations in the Middle East.

The American Secretary of State's visit has been made at an inopportune moment. Coming after yet another Israeli surprise move: the annexation of the Golan Heights and her stubborn insistence on granting no further concessions, it would be wishful thinking to expect a solution to the problem.

The question that comes to mind is – on what grounds should any optimism be based when almost all Middle East negotiations till today have failed to bring together all the parties concerned?

If the problem is that of Palestinian autonomy, the Palestinians should take part in the negotiations. Unfortunately, not only are the Palestinians out of the discussions concerning their future, they have rarely seen eye to eye on the elements of negotiations tabled by Egypt which claims to represent the Arab cause.

While the Palestinians do not recognize Israel, the Jews on their part, have not yet accepted the principle by which Palestinians should be granted any autonomy.

The Irony of these conflicting views held by parties which should have been discussing together but are not, is disheartening and puts back to square one any autonomy.

It is clear that if any head way is going to be made as regards this issue, the rules of the game have to be changed and drastically too. These changes should be deep-rooted and based on a genuine desire by the parties concerned to move from negotiations to much more concrete goals.

Real change in the Middle East means genuine acceptance by Israelis and Palestinians of each other's right to exist. Only after such a framework has been laid, can all the parties get down to real and meaningful discussions.

Otherwise, the innumerable missions like the recent trip to the Middle East by Alexander Haig will remain unnecessary and meaningless diplomatic exercises.

Ben Bongang

48

Cameroon Report 21/03/82: Cameroon's Position on SADR'S Admission into the O.A.U

Introduction: *The seven-year old Western Sahara war seems to be spreading from the battlefield to the corridors of the Organisation of African Unity- OAU, following a decision by the organisation's Secretary-General, Edem Kodjo to admit the Sahrawi Arab Democratic Republic, SADR, of the Western Sahara into the OAU. The decision convulsed the proceedings of the 39th OAU ministerial conference. Morocco, which denies the Polisario Front's SADR government the right to represent the Western Sahara, walked out of the conference, accompanied by eighteen sympathisers including Cameroon. The Yaounde government has issued a statement on its position on the issue, a position which Sam-Nuvala Fonkem now explains unequivocally:*

There has been mounting controversy among political analysts and observers over Cameroons declared position on the Western Sahara question. The debate has been lively and heated particularly because of what appears to be a contradiction in the stated principles that underlay Cameroon's position and the fact that we seldom make public declarations on pertinent issues except those that directly stand as a threat to the political ideology and system we uphold.

The official declaration this week on Cameroon's position on the Western Sahara question bears no contradiction and is quite in line with the mainstream of its conduct in foreign policy. Many observers always fall into the habit of categorising our foreign policy as "moderate" – a label which has now become a euphemism for conservative.

The fact is that although our position on the Western Sahara may not appeal to so-called progressive elements, it is however based on fundamental principles and beliefs which go a long way to account for our own political stability and economic growth. Ours is an ideology guided by moderation, caution and guarded optimism.

The government has made it clear that we are not opposed to the right of peoples to self-determination and independence, but we insist on the agreed political process for the achievement of these rights. Any attempt to interpret our position as being in favour of monarchism or feudalism would be dangerous postulation since our political system is self evident of what we uphold.

It is Cameroon's conviction that OAU principles and resolutions be respected in order to give the organisation its due respect and importance. Any attempt to disregard or undermine the role of the OAU can only lead to the destruction of African unity which we all agree is vital in our struggle against foreign imperialism and the achievement of a new world order.

Granted that Morocco's refusal to negotiate with the active party concerned in the Western Sahara conflict has not facilitated the search for a peaceful solution, the sporadic admission of the Polisario Front into the OAU has made the situation even worse than ever before particularly as there are strong indications that the OAU is on the verge of collapse. And if the OAU collapses, neither the conservatives nor the progressives would gain anything. Thus it is of crucial importance for both sides to converge their ideas and rescue the OAU from an undesirable disintegration (since the present crisis appears to be a conflict of generations).

The tradition of the OAU must be respected because no matter how far the organisation evolves, it cannot wield the power and influence expected of it without a strong foundation or tradition as it were.

The OAU Secretary General, by hastening the admission of the Sahrawi Arab Democratic Republic into the organisation, has instead crystallised differences within the organisation and could severely disrupt the forthcoming OAU summit in Tripoli, in which case his act would have perhaps been heroic, but certainly not diplomatic.

The government and people of Cameroon would very much want the people of the Western Sahara to achieve independence, but this should not be done at the expense of African unity. Perhaps we should also add as a word of caution that whatever stand the government takes, care should be taken to ensure that it does not lead to Cameroon's eventual withdrawal from the OAU as this would not serve the cause of African unity and could be interpreted as a pro-Moroccan position and by implication a pro-monarchist attitude.

Sam- Nuvala Fonkem

Cameroon Report 07/07/1982: The 9th Franco-African Summit

Introduction: *Delegates from some forty-two African countries including twenty Heads of State are returning home after attending the 9th Franco African summit in Kinshasa, Zaire. It is too early to say exactly what the summit achieved concretely for its participants. The only likely beneficiary is host President Mobutu Sese Seko who used the occasion to gain some publicity for his sagging regime. Given the imperialistic objectives of the summit, it is a surprise that so many leaders turned out for the meeting. Eric Chinje has these observations:*

It must have been this year's best-kept secret - Africa's surprise package of the eighties. Some forty African leaders of varied political persuasions, we were told, were going to congregate in Zaire, sit together and, according to French President Francois Mitterrand, informally exchange ideas on some of the major issues confronting the continent. My first reaction to news of the event was one of outright incredulity: It could not be true, it could not happen, at least not in 1982. Who could have accomplished such a feat? Was it France? Was it Mitterrand? Was it Mobutu? Was it an African or a French affair?

I felt a little uncomfortable with the news. It had all the trappings of a colonialist decoy. I could almost certainly hear, in the explicatory words of Mr Mitterrand, the voice of some colonial lords, paternalistically informing his overseas subjects that this thing was totally for their own good. Nothing, note you, against President Mitterrand. I am quite aware, as I believe most Africans are, that France's current leader is possibly the best – or is it truest – friend Africa has had for a long time from among the nations of the West. There had to be some sincerity in the whole thing, but coming in the wake of a year of Chad and the Western Sahara, one could not help but see once again, the discomforting but domineering hand of colonialist authority at play.

Given that only nineteen OAU nations finally sat down to talk the issue over! That the Kinshasa gathering would succeed only opens up a bag of disquieting questions: Who is fooling who about African Unity? What does one make of those warm-hearted embraces that African leaders so gregariously exchange each time they meet? Or words like: "my brother, President X or Y?" Who runs Africa? Who really makes things work in this good old Continent?

For answers, we can only turn to the leaders of Africa, to those for example, who attended the Franco-African summit. What convinced them to turn up? Was it in interest of Africa or did they go the Zaire because France wanted them there?

The Pan-Africanist conscience has always stood out against sugar coated pills dished out from "Whiteman contri", and has always urged us to accept with deep scepticism all professions of goodwill from fellows of another skin pigment, be they right-minded white-skinned socialists, or red-neck American reactionaries. This time around, we will take Francois Mitterrand in good faith; we will swallow his words like balls of "garri" bathed in "okro" soup. But it is important that we remember, that African leaders remember that Africans should run their own affairs. That, however difficult it is, however impossible it might seem at the moment, the answer to Africa's problems is in Africa.

Eric Chinje

Cameroon Report 08/08/1982: OAU Deadlock over Western Sahara

Introduction: *Hopes for the formal opening of the 19th OAU summit in Tripoli, Libya have completely dissipated as a last ditch effort to save the conference yesterday failed to obtain the required number of thirty-four participating member-states necessary to form a quorum. It is now clear, as feared, that Tripoli '82 has failed, exposing once again the inability of African states to uphold a united front through dialogue. The split over the Tripoli summit, the deepest spilt in the history of the OAU, has sparked off speculation and heated debates in political and intellectual circles as well as given rise to a number of perplexing questions about the stability and viability of the Pan-African organisation. Despite the split, Africanists think everything should be done to restore dialogue among member states. Victor Epie Ngome indicates that all member states have a moral duty to safeguard the legality of the OAU by promoting an atmosphere of reconciliation, not by failing to sustain dialogue:*

There seems to be two major roads of being talked about: either you succeed, which often requires hard work, or you fail which is easier because it is enough no to make any effort at all.

As far as this kind of energy economics is concerned, Africans seem to be the world's champions, in that they have always chosen the cheapest and shortest path to the front pages – the path of minimum effort.

We have learnt in time how futile it is for us to try to distinguish ourselves technologically or by any of the recognised standards – except perhaps by sending teams to the world cup competition.

And so we easily close one eye and aim a cheap shot at international fame (or notoriety to be more exact) by providing the world with front page stories of political unrest or economic miasma, civil wars, famine and refugee problems.

I was just listening casually to a rather talkative announcer on a radio station that seems to have a lot of credibility in this language, when I heard something like "at a time when even the Eastern and Western blocs are making efforts to co-operate with each other despite their ideological polarity, it turns out that African leaders who need dialogue most, can't even sit down to talk". And he ended with "what a bad year for Africa".

An immediate reaction could have been to ask whether this announcer, and indeed the system that breeds him, are genuinely interested in Africans getting together and talking – trying to solve their problems, most of which are created and perpetuated by some superpowers.

Now, let's look at that statement in the light of another made under the same casual and jocular circumstances by a more obscure but by no means ignorant party. The setting is a workshop in an automobile sales department. The actors are employees in the company. Says one: Hey old boy, are you coming along to Benghazi? Says the other: Oh no, I am afraid I can't. My elder brother says not to. It was, of course futile to ask the redundant question of who these actors were impersonating. I say "redundant" because the circumstance surrounding the abortion of the Tripoli summit have given rise to speculations – some call them malignant, but nobody seems to call them unfounded speculations that the abortion is being financed by a western capital.

We shall, of course, not spend what little time we have trying to witch-hunt who is or isn't on the payroll, but we are worried about proposals like the one from Sudan – that the summit shift venue from Tripoli. And this for two reasons: one because it gives the impression that the Saharawi admission is a cover-up and that the real problem is the man to chair the summit and by giving that impression, it tends to undermine our stance in the matter – which is that we have nothing against any member country of the OAU, nor non-attendance is strictly in defence of the principles of the organisation.

The second reason which worries us is that neither the proponent of the change of venue nor indeed any other member, volunteered to host the summit.

We hate to think that any African country will be led into an unproductive concern for who chairs the OAU, led by Western countries, some of whose leaders don't even know the names of their African counterparts.

That would endorse the old fear that we in Africa don't know where we are headed' or worse still, that though we have been clamouring for self-government since 1960, deep down we are scared of independence.

By the way, and to pursue the thought further, maybe we've got to the point where someone should pluck the courage to define accession to the OAU chair. Is it a matter of persons or of countries? By implication, and to combine the issues again, we need to be careful not to treat the admission of a new OAU member as if it implied the dismissal of an old one.

It seems clear to us that in what concerns this admission, someone over-stepped bounds and this was a long time ago – a long enough time for the institution in question, namely the OAU General Secretariat to admit its fault and leave the admission to those who have the constitutional mandate.

What has not happened is an anomaly which does not, however, justify the sine-die postponement of deliberations on other and more pressing African issue – like the Namibian independence question.

If we recognise that the OAU can admit or refuse to admit members, but does not grant independence, it will become clear how lacking we are in sense of purpose if we allow the Saharawi admission issue to overshadow our other priorities.

We have so much to unite for. Why pay so much attention to one divisive issue?

Both those who went to Tripoli and those who didn't, definitely have good reason for doing as they did. One thing this reporter fears is that by doing nothing, not even talking, we would again be choosing the easy way to the front pages: by failing to sustain dialogue which is the very essence of the OAU

Victor Epie Ngome

Cameroon Report 03/11/1982: Foiled OAU Summit Reconvened

It was definitely with joy and relief that most Africans greeted the recent assurance that the foiled OAU summit was at last going to hold. For some, the joy was made even fuller by the fact that the summit was indeed to hold in Tripoli because the withdrawal of the Saharawi delegations deprived some member countries of their cover-up for staying back – that is those who pretended that the venue was not their objection.

But, as is always the case, this joy has already sprung a leak with the emergence of this haggle over who will take the Chadian seat. And so for the better part of the week, OAU foreign ministers can't make progress in Tripoli because the two Chadians can't be considerate enough to abstain and allow the other problems facing the continent to be examined.

From the previous discussions and special consultations done at the organisation's level, it ought to be clear to Mr. Miskine as well as Habre and Goukouni themselves, that their country's problem is a many headed monster, and that a permanent solution can't come from Tripoli anymore than it did from Nairobi. The OAU does not legitimise governments, it doesn't even have the right to go into the processes by which member countries legitimise their governments – given that the Amins, the Bokassas and Nguemas were accepted and respected as leaders of their countries and in the same measure as the regime that overthrew them.

Unable to sustain a functional rule, whoever is more powerful in OAU sort of keeps shifting recognition to whoever is more powerful in Chad. Not long ago it was Goukouni, and Habre and his men were publicly proclaimed rebels. Today, the rebels with aid from one of the countries that thrive on our conflicts came out more powerful, and the OAU is confused. If, acting only on the spur of the moment, they identify with Habre today, there is no discounting that tomorrow Goukouni can reinforce with the aid of another power and turn the tables – and so a shilly shally OAU will have been caught up in a perpetual merry-go-round.

Members are already walking out of the Tripoli conference as a way of forcing acceptance for their favourite Chadian faction. But rather than resort to blackmail as if some countries had more to lose than others in the event of the OAU breaking down, why not refer to the provisions of the charter? If splits in opinion are to be resolved by vote, then why not just vote considering that no minority ever agrees that the majority was really right.

In this case, the majority seem to favour asking both Chadian delegations to withdraw, which makes sense. Any walk-outs at this conference and the ensuing summit can be interpreted as part of a trick to hold up OAU business. Last time the pretext was the Saharawi question. This time it's Chad. Next it will be Angola – when the Americans shall have used Savimbi to topple Dos Santos – which will surely happen soon if by mistake the Cubans were asked leave.

Again we hope that the timing of George Bush's tour of the "bush" has nothing to do with the upcoming summit i.e. selling his country's anti-Qadafism to gullible African leaders is right.

This is where, whatever the Libyan leader maybe doing wrong, he is right in insisting that African problems be left to Africans-with no promptings from outside. Just look at the wires, at the bleak projections and misinterpretations, at the sheer propaganda in the western news dispatches, and you know Qaddaffi was right even in asking non African journalists and diplomats to stay away from the conference. After all, how many African journalists and diplomats attend European parliamentary sessions, OAS meetings and so on?

If the Chadians would rather cut one another's throat than try to reconcile and begin national reconstruction, if they would rather drive the wedge on OAU business than join in the search for solutions to the continent's other pressing problems, this is no reason for all African countries to mix up their priorities.

We have pressing economic problems, like the pricing of our commodities, which require that we arrive at a common stand soon. We have the improvement of trade and communication among African countries as a priority. We have the harmonisation of our attempts to acquire technology which is an emergency. We have racists raping us in the south of the continent- with the help of Zionists and imperialists. This is an emergency.

When we have such formidable common enemies to fight against, that's not the time to split into camps behind two blood brothers who refuse to tidy up their house.

And in what concerns South Africa, it is a shame that because of our proneness to division – because of pure centrifugal tendencies, we have not all been able to stand up in unison against the enemy and his allies. And it will be yet a greater shame if even an African leader will be fooled into accepting that the Cuban withdrawal from Angola be part of the dishonest package deal for Namibian independence. Thank goodness, the seller of such a doctrine is not coming to Cameroon.

And we are sure if he came, he would have no audience. In the same respect, a front on which a well-calculated onslaught is sure to produce results is the church. Everywhere the great traveller in the Vatican goes, he condemns apartheid and the illegal occupation of Namibia. Yet the church has never thrown its massive spiritual weight into bringing the racists to reason. Maybe the church needs a push from OAU – unless all African Catholics together, mean less to the pope than a few whites in South Africa.

For this and other urgent reasons, one can't help asking these Africans still dragging their feet to hurry and go to Tripoli and get some concrete work going together. It's been waiting too long.

Victor Epie Ngome

52

Cameroon Report 13/01/1985: Checking the African Dependency Syndrome

Introduction: *Imperialism is manifested within political and economic circles. Politically, governments are tied down through the presence of so-called technical and military advisers. Some currencies are pegged to so-called mother currencies to ensure economic subordination. Ill-conceived military and other agreements are signed to let in what is known in French as "coopérants" who are often less qualified than nationals. Multi-nationals keep exerting pressure on governments so as to drain all money and exploit all the country's wealth. Of late, it seems hopes could be rising because some African governments are gradually realizing the source of their under-development, as our commentator, Fai Henry Fonye observes in the following paper:*

During the week under analysis, the Ivory Coast government announced that it would soon cut back the number of its foreign experts- who are mainly French. One top official said that no less than 90% of the expatriates would have left by 1986. The present number of experts in the Ivory Coast is around 40.000.

The immediate question we want to ask is why does the government of the Ivory Coast want to repatriate these experts? Well, the answers are there. (1) The government is under pressure to cut back on expenses and to promote the employment of Ivorians. (2) Some experts think that they are irreplaceable whereas they are often little more than advisers, or simple bureaucrats. (3) The experts who are recruited

197

either through consultancy firms or directly are considerably more expensive than the technical assistants of coopérants of the host country.

Ivory Coast had financial problems which led to a rescheduling of its medium term external debt last year and growing unemployment among educated young Ivorians has accelerated the phasing out of both privately recruited and government sponsored foreign experts.

The question we may ask at this point is whether the developing world and in particular – Africa, has any lessons to take home from the Ivory Coast? This commentator believes that the answer is a categorical YES.

Many of us would be inclined to say that with all his unpreparedness and his recognized shortcomings, the so-called expert represents a major contribution to development history. For nearly a quarter of a century, we saw experts willing to dirty their hands on the same jobs as ourselves, and having official status into the bargain. In innumerable cases, these people helped to make us feel as part of a wider human community. It does not end there. The good expert learns from the developing country as much as he teaches. Many of these experts will tell you that this mission gave them a new purpose in life. And it is very common for an expert to ask for an extension of his mission; there are even proposals to form a life career.

But let us be objective, for there is another side to the picture. In the Cameroonian context, do we and must we rely on expatriates after 25 years of independence and after instituting our universities and technical institutions which measure well or even beat theirs? A high proportion of these expatriates know little or nothing of the culture, historical background and ways and thoughts of the people they are to serve.

The good expert tries to adapt himself as he goes along, he learns to listen as well as demonstrate. But not all of them do this. This is illustrated by an anecdote from Chad where an old African observed regrettably that the dust cloud i.e., the dust raised by their passing cars, was all he and his fellow villagers saw of certain visiting experts.

He would not have been surprised to hear that in Niger, some local farmers had succeeded in convincing one mission that it was sinking a well in the wrong place. The Europeans had hydrological data referring to a number of years, but they had not learnt of water movements over a longer cycle which were preserved by African folk memory and which eventually proved to be reliable.

Perhaps examples from our own country might be more illustrative. And this commentator wants to quote examples from his own department of the Ministry of Information and Culture about which he can vouch. Because Radio Buea building was planned abroad by experts, the frontage instead of facing the main road and approach to Bokwaongo in Buea, instead faces a ravine which is supposed to be the behind part of the building. The window of the National Broadcasting House in Yaounde, are airtight because the expert who dreamt them was thinking about a European country and not a country in the tropics.

The antennae of the National Station was at one time supposed to cost tens of millions of francs, but a Cameroonian engineer, who is now of late (Chrysanthus Ndikintum), built one for less than two million francs. The air-conditioners in the national station which went bad some two years ago can only be repaired by the experts who built it, while the equipment there depreciates and the broadcasters suffer in oven heat.

In neighbouring Nigeria, the Eko Bridge, a feat of engineering, was built by Nigerians themselves. The difficult Kumba-Mamfe road another marvel of engineering was constructed by Cameroonian engineers although that beautiful road was allowed to go bad and impassable by the old regime and thus insulated the hitherto enterprising people of Mamfe.

Our belief in the expert or expatriate has caused our own experts or technicians and engineers to go into their cocoons. That is why one can hardly recognise an engineer in Cameroon because instead of wearing the usual shorts and working on the road or in factory, he is found in a well cut suit, smoking and telling stories in an office. Where does this inferiority complex come from? Why is it that we talk about independence on paper and not in ideas and deeds?

It is time we realised that the maintenance of expatriates is expensive in many ways. It fosters unemployment in the country. They ask too much for very little achieved. And above all, some of them are engaged in espionage and destabilisation instead of helping us to progress.

Certainly, we need experts. But let us be sure that we do not have our own children who can do the work and even better before hiring the expatriates. There is no place for luxury. There must be the creation of more equal opportunities. We, in the developing world cannot continue to ape along like buffoons.

As for Cameroon, this is the time to let the world see and appreciate what is really new in the New Deal. Some of these things should be independence and self reliance because we have the resources – both natural and human, at least after 25 years of independence. It is unquestionable that the disorder in Africa today is due primarily to a conscious scheme of exploitation by the imperialist countries – a scheme that cannot be dissociated from the nefarious manipulations of the theory of civilization and racial differences. Let those inconsequential experts go and give a chance to our own children.

Fai Henry Fonye

Cameroon Report 02/02/85: The O.A.U. Drought Fund

Introduction: *O.A.U. interim Secretary-General, Peter Onu threw a bombshell this week when as he announced that only two African countries had so far contributed to the much applauded drought fund. Charles Landzeh examines reactions to drought in Africa so far, and charges that African leaders are failing in their responsibilities to the continent, thus perpetrating neo-colonialism:*

When African heads of state decided to establish a fund to help drought victims on the continent at last November's OAU summit in Addis Ababa, observers quickly applauded the decision as a mature one taken by responsible leaders who wanted to save their fellow countrymen from starving to death. But OAU interim Secretary-General Peter Onu shocked those who care about the welfare of Africa and its peoples with a revelation last week that only two countries, Libya and Algeria have so far contributed to the OAU drought fund with no indications of any contributions at hand.

Since the establishment of the OAU drought fund, the real action seems to be taking place outside the continent to help Africa's drought and famine victims and the obvious question again is whether Africa, twenty-five years after independence will still continue to look elsewhere for it problems to be solved.

Already, the World Bank, in the course of the week, assembled aid donors in Paris who pledged the sum of over

One billion dollars to help Africa's dying population. As usual the donors present in Paris were those who dictate policies to the black continent with the few African representatives only cheering from the observer's bench.

Meantime, as African leaders keep on dragging their feet in utter confusion and suffering from the popularity or unpopularity of their paper decision, hundreds of thousands of their countrymen continue dying from famine each day as Africa continues to bury its dead.

As if to challenge African statesmen, African musicians abroad, musicians of African origin, have taken the lead in fund raising. A group of British musicians kicked-off the series with a hit song *"Do they know it's Christmas"* and the sales proceeds projected in millions of dollars, will all be channelled to drought victims in Africa.

In the United States, leading musicians led by Michael Jackson and Lionel Richie, together with about forty other stars have also released a track *"We are the World"*, whose proceeds will go to Africa's drought victims.

Cameroon's Manu Dibango is also leading dozens of Paris- based African stars in that same direction.

With Africa's sons and daughters abroad responding in a timely manner to the sorry situation of their brothers and sisters, there is utter confusion and indecision on the minds of African leaders on the continent.

Although such a move is commendable as it would save more lives, it is also an indication of lack of co-ordination among African leaders. Could it be that Gabon has no confidence in the fund which it approved or that the OAU drought fund has simply been dumped to give room for individual action? Whatever the case, the facts are there on the ground-thousands of Africans are dying every other day from lack of food and water and it should be the concern of all African statesmen.

Whether voted into office by the ballot or by the barrel of the gun, each and every African leader has an inescapable responsibility i.e. that of guaranteeing the welfare of its citizens at all times, by trying to solve the continent's problems firstly, before looking elsewhere for assistance.

If the far- fetched slogan "Africa for Africans" has to come nearer each day towards reality, African leaders must try to close those avenues of neo-colonialism now more than ever before or it will be too late.

Charles Landzeh

54

Cameroon Report 03/03/85: The Western Sahara Ten Years After

Introduction: *Abroad, events have kept following up each other's heels as if the end of the world is in the horizon. In the Maghreb region, Algeria accepted to participate in a proposed summit meeting on condition that all questions are raised and discussed. The Sahrawi Arab Democratic Republic indicated that it would not be in the logic of history and time to hold such a summit meeting without their participation. This could be certainly understood because time can never go backwards, just as the cycle of historical development is continuous and cannot be reversed. King Hassan II of Morocco yesterday celebrated his country's national day not where he originally wanted. Observers speculated that the change might have been for security reasons. But all these coincide with the 10th anniversary of Morocco's annexation of the Western Sahara after Mauritania gave up its share of the territory. As the occasion enters the annals of Western Saharan history, it is today entering the annals of Cameroon Report's history through a chronological analysis by Charles Landzeh:*

Ten years ago, in 1975, Spain surprisingly abandoned its colonial territory of Western Sahara with no formula or structures for the independence or self-government of its inhabitants.

King Hassan II of Morocco, in what went down in African modern history as the Green March, quickly sent thousands of his citizens to occupy the northern part of the abandoned desert territory. Mauritania, in what turned out to be a short-lived ambition, also occupied the southern part of Western Sahara to join Morocco as African colonial masters of the 20th century.

Such developments which sealed the legitimate hopes of a people traumatised and oppressed for centuries by the Spanish colonial machine only generated a militant nationalist spirit among the little known Polisario liberation movement.

Polisario made its mark in 1976, when amidst running battles against Morocco, it declared the occupied Western Sahara an independent country officially called the Saharan Arab Democratic Republic (S.A.D.R.).

The long, controversial and explosive political history of Polisario's SADR, backed by Algeria alongside a desert war with Morocco took a new dimension when SADR gained the most expensive admission yet into the Organisation of African Unity late last year.

King Hassan II, in a record-breaking reaction, pulled the Kingdom of Morocco out of the Pan-African body to open another page in the political history of continent.

Ten years since the Green March was organised and twenty-four years since coming to power in Morocco, King Hassan II planned to celebrate his anniversary in El Alhoun, capital city of the occupied Western Sahara this week.

The choice of El Alhoun seemed to be no accident whatsoever in the questioning minds of African political commentators and observers. Was Morocco challenging or playing down the OAU's recognition and admission of Polisario's SADR into its fold?

Was it a show of the Kingdom's politico-military might to heavily water down Polisario's resounding diplomatic victory achieved in Addis Ababa last year? Did King Hassan II choose El Alhoun just to remind those who care that he was in control of the vital part of the occupied territory which now has the status of an independent country?

The choice of El Alhoun could simply be another provocative act against Polisario since Rabat has repeatedly thrown overboard all international attempts for a negotiated settlement in the ten-year old desert war.

Whatever the case, King Hassan's plans to celebrate his twenty-four years of rule in El Alhoun have been abandoned in a last minute decision following an upsurge of military activities by Polisario. The liberation fighters shot down a West German war plane over SADR earlier in the week and promised similar actions against any one violating its territorial sovereignty.

Although Rabat has not explained the sudden change of venue, there is little doubt that Polisario's war signals have been well received by the Monarch who would not celebrate twenty-four years of power with guns rumbling in the background. It is also apparent that the change of venue could have come from pressure from foreign dignitaries invited to the feast.

While Polisario cannot readily claim victory for the sudden change of venue, the significant message it is sending to Rabat is that time has proved its worth as the most effective weapon against colonisation and that sooner or later Morocco will walk out of Western Sahara in what, this time, could be the *Yellow March*.

Charles Landzeh

Cameroon Report 21/04/85: South Africa: Botha's Lame Reforms

Introduction: *Racist South African authorities this week, delivered what appeared to be the most conciliatory package in decades to resolve the apartheid question and to promote the search for Namibian independence from South Africa. This package comprised the abolition of the immorality and mixed marriages acts which prevented love or marriage across the races, and a projected withdrawal of racist forces of oppression from southern Angola. Our African affairs observer, Charles Landzeh looks at how far such a package can be delivered, and how far it could solve the problem of Namibian independence:*

In two volleys, Pretoria announced the abolition of the immorality and mixed marriages acts which prevented love or marriage across the races, and closely followed up with a statement to withdraw South African occupation forces from southern Angola.

While it is easy to see Pretoria's move as a precipitated response to mounting anti-apartheid pressures from sympathizers in the United States and open disinvestment threats from the rest of the world, many questions abound as to what the real intentions of Pretoria are in making such a quick move for the first time since apartheid became an official policy in 1948.

Apartheid or separate development of races has been institutionalised in South Africa by a series of acts and laws. The immorality and mixed marriages acts legally forbid love or marriage across the races, the group areas act provides for the establishment of separate residential areas for the different races, while the pass laws regulate the movement of people from one residential area to another and who must carry along passes or official permits.

Apartheid therefore is based on a chain of acts and laws and the abolition of one or two of these acts would have no meaning unless the whole file is done away with.

For example, how can people make love and get married when they cannot move freely in and out of each other's residential areas or meet without fear? This explains why anti-apartheid leaders have quickly dismissed the abolition of the immorality and mixed marriages acts as another ploy by Pretoria to fool the rest of the world.

In sum, President Botha's abolition of the immorality and mixed marriages acts amounts to the provision of sentimental liberties to the races which have little or no significant impact on the anti-apartheid struggle.

What the rest of Africa and peace loving nations want are well-meaning reforms which would give majority rule and a one man one vote legal institution in South Africa. President Botha's sentimental liberties could be another soft move to dampen the rising fervour of the anti-apartheid struggle which is now taking greater proportions and threatening the very foundations of that hated inhuman system on the continent.

In another statement, Pretoria announced it was withdrawing all its occupation forces from southern Angola with immediate effect.

Although President Pieter Botha gave explanation why such a move was coming fourteen months behind the Lusaka agreements with Angola, subsequent statements have revealed Pretoria's true intentions.

Those who care about developments in Southern Africa were still thinking hard on the withdrawal plans when Pretoria unleashed its project to set up a puppet transitional government in Namibia without the participation of the South West Africa people's Organisation (SWAPO), the sole and legitimate liberation movement recognised by the OAU and the United Nations in the struggle for Namibia's independence.

Pretoria's announced withdrawal from southern Angola therefore turned out to be a pre-emptive manoeuvre to win whatever support it can for its evil plans in Namibia which it has continued to occupy and exploit in open defiance of world opinion.

President Botha's evil package for Namibia, in all, is a slap on the face of the United Nations as it completely ignores UN resolution 435 calling for supervised elections in the South West African territory with the immediate pullout of the racist South African forces.

Racist South Africa geographically has no territorial boundaries with Angola but the presence of its forces in the independent country can only be explained by the fact that Pretoria violated Namibian and Angolan territories with impunity in its cross-border raids.

In 1983, the racist forces invaded southern Angola from its solidified bases in the Caprivi Strip of northern Namibia to support UNITA rebels against Angola's legitimate government and stayed on permanently. The occupation forces have been carrying out search and destroy operations against SWAPO fighters in that region.

Practically, therefore, South African forces are simply moving back to their base in northern Namibia on the frontiers with Angola, their position in 1983 and would continue its stubborn tradition of cross-border raids on Angola.

South African troop withdrawal from southern Angola is still meaningless unless it leads to Namibia's independence.

The South West Africa People's Organisation celebrated twenty-five years of it troubled existence on April 19 with no fruitful end to its liberation struggle in sight. In fact, SWAPO's Central African representative Nguno Wakolece said in Yaounde recently that Africa was doing very little beyond political rhetoric to help the SWAPO liberation fighters. Pretoria seems to be tossing the entire continent at will. With the Nkomati and Lusaka agreements yawning in the backyard, the racists have come up this time with another diabolical plan for Namibia. The challenges seem to be unending and the question now is for how long will Pretoria continue dragging the rest of the continent by the nose with impunity?

Charles landzeh

56

Cameroon Report 16/06/85: African Leaders in Europe

Introduction: *Last week, we received a letter from one of our listeners in Wum, working with the Delegation of Agriculture, who wanted us to explain to him why some African leaders, including ours are received at European airports by junior ministers while others are received by heads of state and government. Our observer of African affairs, Charles Landezh took up time to investigate and has this commentary for Cameroon Report, on the protocol issue raised by the reception of African leaders in Europe:*

The nature and quality of the reception given to African leaders visiting European countries often provoke deep and disturbing feelings among the patriotic nationals of the African countries concerned.

Most African leaders are welcomed on arrival by junior ministers, some are lodged in commercial hotels instead of presidential palaces, and their visits at times begin and end with little or no awareness of the masses of the host countries.

Such passive treatment of African leaders abroad contrasts greatly with the enormous and at times unnecessarily exaggerated preparations and welcome ceremonies accorded these European leaders visiting African countries. Special dresses with printed effigies of visiting European leaders, organised mobilisation of the masses on the road sides and a temporary halt to the nation's productive machinery are part of the reception ceremonies given to our august visitors.

It is this contrasting phenomenon which took Cameroon Report into the office of the protocol service of our Ministry of Foreign Affairs for an explanation.

Protocol officials say visits are categorized into official, state or working and private, with official visits being considered as the most important and engaging.

Official visits go with red carpet treatment and twenty-one gun salute and in the case of France, the President himself comes to the airport to welcome the visitor who also has a right to a presidential palace and other honours. The working or state visit enjoys a lesser welcoming ceremony with a minister on hand at the airport and lesser honours.

What were not adequately explained was the criteria for determining either an official visit or a working visit, more especially as the press organs often receive communiqués talking of official working visits.

The protocol service however gave some food for thought when it said that in the case of France, a strong political tie between the two countries or even the personality of the African leader may help boost the rating of the visit as official in which case the French leader will be on hand at the airport.

Now the very first observation here is that very few African leaders visiting France especially from its former colonies have had that privilege to be welcomed by the French president which is directly the opposite of what happens when the French leaders visit African countries. (Last year, a West African Francophone country even bought uniforms for university students to greet a visiting French President).

Another observation is that some African leaders waited for their visits to be classified as official in vain for such a long time that they adopted strong arm and even threatening political tactics to gain their cause. It is the case of Cameroon's southern neighbour who was received by his Paris counterpart for the first time since independence recently.

In 1983, a young French speaking African head of state boycotted a dinner at the Elysée palace to protest the level of reception given to him at the airport which was incompatible with his status as head of state.

Some African leaders with opposing ideologies are even said to have come neck-to-neck in a hotel in a Paris suburb because they were lodged together during separate and unannounced visits.

The big question is why does this protocol treatment of heads of state remain only one-way? While it is true that most African leaders visiting Europe go on a begging trip, the universal fact is that a head of state is the same and should be treated with all the honours as it is the case with those visiting Africa. The pride and honour of a given country goes along with its leader everywhere he finds himself whether on a official or a working visit and cannot be undermined by it former colonial masters.

The paternalistic relationships of colonial times had to give way after independence to a shoulder to shoulder co-operation between Africa and Europe in international relations. It would appear this is still a long way ahead as Africans still witness their pride of independence and sovereignty minimised on several fronts.

The fact, though inadmissible, is only a bitter reminder of neo-colonialism described by a leading African statesman as "going out from the front door, coming in from behind".

Charles Landzeh

Cameroon Report 23/6/1985: South Africa's puppet Government in Namibia

Introduction: *Over the week, the criminal racist regime in South Africa erected a puppet clique in Windhoek, Namibia so as to prolong their stay and exploitation of the people. Our African affairs observer, Charles Landzeh examines this move and indicates that force is the only way out of this colonial situation in Southern Africa:*

Decades of the controversial independence struggle in Namibia took a new twist earlier in the week when the arrogant and headstrong racist regime in Pretoria installed a puppet government in Windhoek, the Namibian capital.

In fact, the puppet gang is a fragile and artificial rainbow coalition of Pretoria's stooges handpicked from unpopular backyard parties in Namibia which owe their existence to racist South Africa and not to Namibians. The SWAPO (South West Africa People's Organisation) is out of Pretoria's list. However the event carried its own significance in Africa's pre and post colonial contemporary history.

For the second time in two decades, Africa witnessed what has come to be known as (Unilateral Declaration of Independence) in southern Africa. It was in 1965 when rebel leader, Ian Smith unilaterally declared northern Rhodesia (now Zimbabwe) independent from Great Britain but the British stunned the rest of the world with silence and impotence towards the revolt, unlike the case with India in the 1940s.

It has happened again in 1985 with racist South Africa staging its one man show in Namibia in the face of the international community with impunity.

What is provocative in Pretoria's action is that it comes on the heels of criminal raids and spying missions into neighbouring independent Botswana and Angola, together with the growing massacres of blacks inside the racist bastion. But perhaps of greater significance is that Pretoria's action comes in the heart of heated debates at the United Nations on the Namibian question.

In 1978, the United Nations adopted resolution 435 calling for a ceasefire and withdrawal of South African occupation forces and the organisation of United Nations-supervised elections in Namibia. For seven years, the UN resolution has eroded in the face of Pretoria's arrogance, the different plans and activities of the so-called Western Contact Group, the front-line states, and the U.S. of constructive engagement towards Pretoria.

If there is to be any forward movement in Namibia's troubled history, the UN must re-examine resolution 435 which has now been over-taken by Pretoria with last Monday's puppet government in Windhoek. There should be a forceful rejection of the puppet setup and a reprisal against the headstrong BOTHA clique for openly and repeatedly defying the United Nations. This could be an additional clause providing for immediate practical sanctions on the Pretoria clique by all UN member states.

While it is true that South Africa's western backers would not go further than verbal and demagogic condemnations at the UN, the entire Third World still has the alternative of throwing its weight behind SWAPO in its intensified armed struggle against the racist. It was the case behind the successes of FRELIMO in Mozambique, the MPLA in Angola, PAIGC in Guinea and Cape Verde, and the FLN in Algeria.

African and other third world countries which have lived through the pains of colonialism must draw lessons from their own experiences that the United Nations Organisation has often succeeded elsewhere in other issues but not in granting independence to colonized territories.

The devil is the United Nation's Security Council where the privileged members often manifest an unwillingness to act positively on Third World issues due to senseless super power rivalries and vested selfish interests.

Charles Landzeh

58

Cameroon Report 14/7/1985: Africa's Troubled Politics

Introduction: *Many observers of African politics agree that the military can never be a saviour even as civilian leaders continue to be corrupt. No military government has yet succeeded in fulfilling promises made after over-throwing a civilian regime. The recently foiled, though bloody, attempt to seize power in Guinea by a faction of the military once more demonstrated the fragility of leadership in Africa. Our international affairs observer, Ben Bongang now looks at some of the causes of political instability on the continent:*

It ought to constitute a real cause for worry to us that bloody violence should make changes in the leadership of post-independent African countries.

Almost to a country, the prospect of a change of power, even when this is constitutional, creates an atmosphere of deep apprehension. This peculiar character has made political discussion taboo and a potentially dangerous subject even within academic circles.

The general tendency among many is to attribute today's ills to the colonial past and to the fact that almost three decades after independence, most of the countries on the continent take the cue for their leadership changes from former European colonial masters.

While this premise cannot be discounted given the rather intimate economic and military agreements that tie Africa to her European masters, it must also be agreed that the source of most of the chaos can be found on the continent itself.

If the driving force of politics everywhere is the ambition to make a mark by one's contribution to the history of a nation through transforming ideological concepts into concrete acts for the good of all, in Africa, the personal ambition that motivates its sons often falls short of these noble ideals to espouse mundane desires like the accumulation of wealth and power. And it is at the end of such leadership that the country learns of their leader's wealth locked up in foreign bank accounts.

Though the craving for wealth is important, the tribal origins of the leaders often are a factor of key importance. The tribe indirectly constitutes the power base, a constituency from which the key personalities of the country must come. This tribal factor is prominent in countries with few and large ethnic groupings like in Zimbabwe, Guinea, Nigeria, Sudan and others. It often constitutes the source of discontent when one tribe is pitted against the others as examples of recent years on the continent confirm.

At the dawn of African independence and with the massive return home of the intelligentsia trained abroad to replace the school teachers and trade unionists who were at the vanguard of politics, hopes for better times were raised. Within almost three decades, the crop of university graduates has massively mushroomed on the continent.

Unfortunately, their score card so far leaves much to be desired; the back-stabbing that was the feature of much of the continent's politics in the earlier days has taken on even more alarming proportions today. The trooping from the barracks of soldiers to seize power is proof of the death in the leadership potential of the African intelligentsia. But sadly enough, because soldiers are untrained in the art of civilian politics, their record so far has been dismal with rival factions within the armies taking turns in bloody power confrontations.

Most observers of African politics say the problems stem from the flexibility of constitutions. To them, the manipulation of constitutions to consolidate personal power from one leader to the other, or worse, the total shoving aside of this document in the case of the military, is at the root of the ill. Closely associated to the constitutional factor, they cite the muzzling of the press. The press which ought to serve as a bridge between the leadership and the people is at best relegated to the rear to perform the role of mouth piece of government.

Such a press in a country with a weak judiciary and a rubber stamp legislature indicates the consolidation of absolute power within the executive. Without the checks and balances these institutions could provide, the cycle of violence becomes the order of the day. And that unfortunately is the lot of a good number of African countries at the end of the 20th century.

Ben Bongang

Cameroon Report 18/8/1985: Pope John Paul II in Africa

Introduction: *Cameroonians will host Pope John Paul II for their first time next week-end. He will also be the first ever pope to visit Cameroon, though this would be his third visit to Africa. Preparations are reaching fever-pitch with the erection of podia in all the four Ecclesiastic provinces of the country. Before we ever see him and know what message he has for Cameroonians, our African affairs observer, Charles Landzeh has this view on the pope's relations with Africa:*

The repeated papal visits to Africa (1980, 1982, and 1985) are seen as Vatican's great concern over the changing trends of the Catholic Church in Africa which observers say is steadily going through a quiet and disturbing revolution.

Churches, especially in the rural areas, are gradually adapting their Catholicism to meet African conditions with messages drawing on African socio-cultural and religious realities. Aspects such as polygamy, rejected by the Vatican, are no longer enough to throw a Christian out of the church as they are part of the African traditional setting.

African languages are very much present during church services as God in no longer deemed in Africa to understand only Latin. African songs, drums, dance and symbols as well as the use of traditional dresses and even crying are common place in African Christian churches today.

The Vatican has not yet found a place for the ancestral spirits which are part and parcel of every African traditional home, a source of comfort, guidance and moral authority. Rome has repeatedly dismissed African beliefs in the possession of spirits as primitive pragmatism. African traditional beliefs and the worship of ancestral spirits which had for long been suppressed by the Vatican resurfaced through the traditional radicalism of Bishop Patrick Kalilombe of Malawi in 1976 and especially of Archbishop Emmanuel Milingo of Zambia last year. He provoked worldwide concern and controversy among the Catholics by holding huge healing ceremonies and mass exorcisms throughout Zambia.

Zaire, the heart land of Catholicism in Africa where half of the country's thirty-three million people are Catholics is of special concern and is said to be openly taking initiative away from Rome with a heavy dose of African traditions being injected into the Catholic Church. Powerful independent churches enjoying a large autonomy from the Roman Catholic Church have also developed in Kenya and Ethiopia.

Papal fears and suspicions have also been expressed that Marxism might be injected into Catholic thinking in Africa and pope John Paul II warned last year against what he described as 'liberation theology and campaign for social justice in Africa based on class distinction and class struggle'.

Observers say the Vatican's past dogmatic attitude towards the drift of Catholicism in Africa to its traditional setting is widely responsible for the current radical and revolutionary trends of some Catholic churches on the continent.

Critics say the Vatican has been too reluctant in understanding and conceding to African cultural trends in relation with the Catholic Church in Africa.

Pope John Paul's repeated trips to Africa are therefore seen as a tireless effort by a church leader who is determined to keep the sixty-six million African Christians within the fold of the world's 815 million Catholics.

The Holy pontiff has already talked of meaningful change within the Catholic Church in Africa for the first time; a statement which would likely please many Catholics on the continent. The quiet revolution of the Catholic Church in Africa is embracing both the African tradition and Christianity, and this represents a powerful religious phenomenon which the Vatican can no longer ignore.

Pope John Paul II's 27th visit abroad is also taking him to Morocco, an Islamic state and given the fragility of the Catholic Church in the face of Islam in the Sahelian belt of Africa, the Pope's stop-over in Rabat might mean something more than just a pleasure trip.

Charles Landzeh

Cameroon Report 03/11/1985: Leadership Succession in Africa

Introduction: *Next Tuesday, November 5, the new Tanzanian President Ali Hassan Mwinyi, will be sworn in as the new leader of that East African state. It will mark the beginning of a new era and an end to Julius Nyerere's reign which dominated the country's first quarter of a century since independence in 1961. By transferring power, President Nyerere is doing what few African leaders would readily accept because it means leaving the trappings of power and the lime-light of attention. In Cameroon Report today, our international affairs observer, Ben Bongang uses the opportunity of the changing of the guard in Tanzania, to comment on this singular African style succession:*

Stepping down from power freely by African leaders is such a rare happening, so the apparent smooth transfer of government in Tanzania must be greeted as a great act of courage by veteran statesman Mwalimu Julius Nyerere.

On the basis of his own merit, Nyerere receives high marks for his performances. By African current standards he is one of the least controversial leaders who consistently during his reign was instrumental in forging Third World and African opinions within the non-aligned movement, the Commonwealth and on issues like southern Africa.

Perhaps his greatest legacy will be his modesty and frankness, rare qualities with people wielding power. Rising from the lowly position of school teacher to that of head of state, he espoused a brand of socialism whose results, he

231

acknowledges today, are far below expectation. Nevertheless, he has learnt to adjust to the changing tide of times.

Nyerere's personal decision to hand over power, though rare, is not the first of its kind, nor would it be the last time a long reigning resident assumes upon himself the powers of anointing a heir. It is a trend that probably would continue so long as the transition is smooth and peaceful. In Senegal and Cameroon, the exercise of power transfer was conducted with varying results. In Sierra Leone, the grand old man Siaka Stevens hand-picked major-General Joseph Momoh as his own successor. His choice of a soldier, though surprising to many, could be a strategy to defuse any restlessness from the barracks since soldiers would readily identify with Major-General Momoh.

Another elderly African statesman, Houphouet Boigny of the Ivory Coast defied all speculations regarding the choice of a successor and instead sought and acquired yet another presidential term of office for himself. President Boigny's argument so far is that if a successor were named, the person would become the target for all the attacks of his jealous peers. The Ivorian leader has opted instead for a free for all race for the presidency in case of a vacancy, with the president of the national assembly organising the contest. How smoothly all this works out in practice when the time comes is anybody's guess. The Guinean soldiers led by General Lansana Conte did not give room for such an exercise in their own country.

Meanwhile, in Liberia, another curious exercise in democracy aimed at bringing back the country to civilian rule has just been organised and won by former Master-Sergeant Samuel Doe now a five-star General, who, five years ago with a group of friends from the barracks, shot his way to power in an exceptionally bloody coup d'état.

No sooner were results of the elections proclaimed than accusations of rigging by the opposition parties were heard. To them, Doe is "a player who is an umpire in the same game". However strong their protests, it is unlikely that it would affect Doe and his supporters.

By standing as candidate in civilian elections, President Doe definitely did not want a repetition of the Ghanaian situation where Flight Lieutenant Jerry Rawlings handed over power to a civilian president Hilla Limann just to turn around and seize it again. All these examples, by all means far from exhaustive, are indicative of an endemic problem in African politics-that of succession.

While some people would go for the dynastic style inheritance where the ruling leader chooses the heir who is sole candidate for presidency, there is the Liberian multi-party option even though the problem of rigging still looms large. It would be ill advised to attempt to prescribe the best pattern for leadership transition. Whichever form a country opts for, the role of the population should be made more important.

The impression one gathers is that the leadership treats the people in these succession issues as an almost irrelevant factor. Since, after all, decisions have been taken by the leadership, the population almost as an afterthought, is then cajoled into endorsing the sole candidate. The results of the polls are hardly ever below 99%.

Ben Bongang

Cameroon Report 11/11/1985: Reagan-Gorbachev Summit

Introduction: *The Geneva summit meeting between U.S. President Ronald Reagan and Soviet leader, Mikhail Gorbachev is the first super power summit in six years. It means a meeting of the highest producers of all sorts of arms, both for so called defence and business. These two countries have never fought against each other directly but they have made the world restless than it was between 1909 and 1945. Yet the buyers are only those who ironically cannot manufacture combine-harvesters for home agriculture. What should these buyers do when the producers start talking about arms control? We put this question to our African observer, Charles Landzeh:*

As the dust raised by the US-Soviet talks in Geneva settles, there seems to be a happy feeling worldwide that wider avenues for co-operation, peaceful coexistence between the East and the West and greater prospects for the reduction of tension between the super powers have been found.

Barely a few days after the Geneva talks, the US and Soviet Union have decided to resume air flights between Washington and Moscow on the heels of what turned out to be the most publicised and the most acclaimed summit by the super power allies in recent times.

With the big guys and major arms manufacturers talking about the reduction of weapons and provide testing grounds for them, Africa ought to feel concerned. For Africa, possibly the greatest dumping found for non-nuclear weapons, the fall out of the Geneva talks should provoke some reflections on disarmament on the continent.

A quick look across the budgetary allocations of most African countries indicates that the expenditure on arms occupies either first or second place on the priority list. Even famine ridden countries have given priority to heavy arms purchases, plunging themselves deeper into debts in the process while other countries spend astronomically on arms, claiming that the best defence is to be well-armed, even during peace time. Such a claim is only ridiculous and easily disqualified as virtually all African countries have established secret or open defence clauses with their various former colonial masters or other industrialised powers. These clauses provide for quick assistance in times of war which shows that African countries cannot defend themselves.

What probably justifies the vast and enormous expenditure on arms is often the desire by African leaders to build permanent and unrestrained personal power. African leaders both civilian and military feel happy and confident behind units armed to the teeth even at the expense of human liberties.

The public parade of the country's military arsenal and massive deployment of the army among the people is often and unnecessary show of force during peace time in a bid to intimidate the people and terrify invisible dissidents.

Because the citizens are often brutalised and their human rights violated in the process, a climate of hostility towards the regime develops spontaneously among the people. The leaders therefore centralise, consolidate and even personalise power in dictatorships of which there are many on the continent.

The Geneva talks between the super powers which seemed to have opened another era of peaceful coexistence and prospects for a reduction of world tension should also provoke a revision of our priorities over the prospects for peace. Those who buy such weapons should also talk peace from their observer benches.

Charles Landzeh

62

Cameroon Report 16/11/1985: Africa and its Elections

Introduction: *It has become fashionable for election results to be rejected by losers in contemporary Africa each time there is a democratic experience in any of the countries on the continent. In most cases the winners claim 99.99% or as of recent a 100% victory at the polls. Our African affairs observer, Charles Landzeh explains that what sometimes contradicts such victory claims are the allegations of rigging and protests from the losers who in most cases are either brutally silenced or simply coerced and manoeuvred into obscurity:*

The unwillingness of those who win such elections to listen at least to the voice of the losers and the brutality with which the opposition is silenced, drives them underground or into exile and subsequently creates an undemocratic situation, in what was intended to a be a democratic experience.

The newly elected or incumbent leaders quickly become dictators of sorts, using all the open or secret methods of suppression in the expensive process to keep power. Some incumbents even organise elections in their own style to proclaim themselves re-elected in the twisted process to stay longer in power.

Now, all these manoeuvres and unholy democratic machinations take place against the backdrop of deep frustrations, anguish and a feeling of deceit among a given population whose aspirations for improved living standards evaporate every other day.

What is even more frustrating is that most incumbents centralise and personalise political power in the hands of one, in what some African political observers have described as the "divine right of presidents" to the detriment of Ministers and collaborators alike.

Such a situation generates mounting discontent among the population and growing detachment from the rulers. The people readily express a willingness to embrace any move which would partially or completely change the present structures.

This is, and has often been, the fertile platform for coups and coup attempts in Africa; the event which is often greeted in the early hours by smiling faces on the streets. Nigeria, Uganda and Liberia are only recent cases of the sad story on the continent in its post colonial political history.

In all these, the African electorate is the big loser. Often the question is whether a voter should go to the polls or not and whether his vote will have any meaning at all. The African voter today would no longer bother himself going to the polling station since he can predict the results of the presidential election. Even in the Ivory Coast where a record 100% was scored in the presidential election or re-election, as it were recently, observers also noted a record low in the voter turnout at the polls.

For many, what was normally seen as an occasion for anyone to freely exercise a civic right and choose a leader of one's judgement in a democratic experience has evaporated. For many, the holding of any elections now more than ever before is tantamount to building platforms for coups or attempted coups in the near or distant future.

Charles Landzeh

www.ingramcontent.com/pod-product-compliance
Lightning Source LLC
Chambersburg PA
CBHW050900300426
44111CB00010B/1322